AS FOR US AND OUR HOUSE

A His & Her Devotional

by

Clinton & Sherri Lindo

DEDICATION

To our wonderful fathers, Clinton Lindo and the late Thomas Moore, who passed during the writing of this book, thank you for your wisdom, strength, and teaching us faith in God. And to our mothers, Janie Moore and the late Theresa Lindo, thank you for your amazing love and encouragement. We are both blessed to have such a legacy to draw from as we parent and grandparent. We dedicate this book to all of you.

TABLE OF CONTENTS

INTRODUCTION

When I graduated college, I bought my first new car. It was a Mazda MX-3, a black sporty model that I became pretty intimate with over the years that followed. That car saw the morning commuter traffic of NYC on many occasions and was also very used to long stretches of I-95. Since I really liked the car, and since I kind of like technical things, I often brought my car manual into the house with me so I can read through it.

As the car began to show its age, I took apart the less-engine-y parts of the car when they needed fixing. I was pretty proud of myself up until the day that my indicator stopped flashing. This had happened before, and it was because a bulb was out and needed replacing. However, it wasn't any of the bulbs this time; all the lights still illuminated, they just no longer flashed. This happened right around the time the car was due for its annual inspection, so I needed to get it fixed. I pored through the manual, but nothing was there that described the problem I was experiencing. This was long before YouTube and Reddit, so on to a mechanic I went. In my younger days, my mechanic selection skills were pretty sub-par, so I ended up in front of three guys who *also* had no idea where the problem was. They took my rear light assembly apart, and when realizing that messing with the bulb and the light socket did nothing, they tried to go deeper into my trunk, resulting in the plastic lining of my trunk being ripped in half.

That visit to the mechanic was more harm than good; but I finally spoke to someone…someone who knew what the problem was and what was needed. It was a flasher component. It was nowhere near the trunk; it actually was located underneath the steering wheel. I ordered a new one, and when it came in, I was able to replace it in under ten minutes. All I could say to myself was, "Wow, I wish I knew about that sooner."

When I first got married and later had children, there were a number of those moments. There was no cut-and-dried manual for me to read from cover to cover; after all, no manual would contain the quirks of my wife and children and how to deal with them. I ran headlong into many problems, made worse by family and friends who still weren't sure about us, and had to muddle through. We talked to people that did not know the solutions to the problem, and just like those mechanics, trying what they suggested did more harm than good. As we began to understand that we needed more knowledge, we frequented marriage seminars and marriage workshops. We ended up in front of people who experienced some of the same problems we were facing and what was needed to fix them. They also pointed us back to the Bible where we had missed solutions that seem as clear as day to us now. We realized that God had the solutions for everything we faced, and through study and prayer, He would reveal them to us. We looked back at all we had learned with the same sentiment, "Wow, we wish we had known this sooner."

When we were inspired with the idea of writing this devotional, we thought about what we didn't know when we first got married and considered what we learned about how to keep a marriage together as well as a family together…not only together, but happy. What would I say to my younger self and other new fathers just starting out? What would my wife say to new wives and mothers?

This devotional is puts into words what we've learned about ourselves, each other, our lives and our expectations. There will undoubtedly be moments when you find yourself nodding along, reading something that you've long known or at least suspected. However, if there is just one moment when you pause and say to yourself, "Wow, I'm glad I learned that now," it will be worth us writing. Our prayer is that this devotional will help you, as well as bring your family closer to each other and closer to Christ. We would love to run

into you on the streets of gold, where we can all
thank Jesus together.

THEME 1 – SETTING THE FOUNDATION

Every well-made home requires a solid foundation. Without that foundation, the house may be built, but it would not be able to withstand any number of adverse conditions, and would eventually fall apart. In the same way, a good family needs to have a strong foundation, and that foundation is Christ. Without Christ as our foundation, any wind of adversity could damage the family beyond repair. This first section of the devotional will help guide you through the "bigger picture" aspects of creating and sustaining a family that serves the Lord. The topics addressed in this theme are Family Dynamic, Family Identity, Family Relationship with Christ and Family Purpose.

THE FAMILY DYNAMIC

Building a house takes a lot of work and requires expertise in a number of different areas. Concrete workers must apply their knowledge in pouring a foundation. Roofers must apply their expertise in covering the house. Electricians must apply their expertise in wiring and electrical work. The jobs that these different professionals perform vary wildly; sometimes, if you watch a building site/project, you'll see different people focusing on different things, going in different directions, tending to their specific tasks. However, one thing that they *do* have in common is what the house will look like when it's completed. Every single one of those professionals has looked at the plans and agreed to work on the project, keeping in mind how the finished product will look.

When we talk about what a family dynamic looks like, this would be a family working toward a common goal or vision that will benefit the family. Just like the builders of a house may have different strengths and expertise, each family member may not all do the same things or in the same way. Family members, just like workers on a building site, employees in a corporation, or church members, have different strengths and talents. What is important is not that everybody thinks exactly the same way – I have greatly benefited from being married to a woman who does not think exactly the way I do – but that everyone focuses on and values the same goals.

As a Christian family, paramount in your goals should be getting to the kingdom. It should be what all your other goals are directly connected to or in harmony with. Besides this very important goal, there might be a focus on getting all the children valuable educations, or maybe on a parent looking to go back to school. It could also be a family ministry of reaching out and helping the community. Whatever it might be, the family should be on the same page. **1 Corinthians 1:10 says, "Now I beseech you, brethren, by the name of our Lord Jesus Christ, that ye speak the same thing, and that there be no division among you; but that ye be perfectly joined together in the same mind and in the same judgement." (KJV)** Those home builders would not be successful if they were looking at different plans for the house. The result of that approach would be a house that would not be of any good use to anybody. By the same token, a family that does not work in harmony and operates in division will benefit only one or two family members, if any at all.

The family dynamic even comes down to day-to-day operations. It is in everybody's best interest to ensure that the household and the family run smoothly. It might look like me taking over the laundry and house cleaning while my wife takes classes. It might look like my son taking over cooking a meal while his parents are working on a project. Whatever it looks like in your house, everyone should be working in harmony with one another. As the father, our job is to set the vision with our wives and call family meetings so that the family can not only buy into the vision, but find their part in it. A good vision benefits every member of the family, and the benefits to each member should be highlighted. Children at an early age must be told that they are valuable members of the family and encouraged to engage in activities that benefit everyone.

Things might not always run smoothly; there might be quite a number of wrenches in your future. However, a family built on this foundation will be able to handle problems and setbacks better than most. If you endeavor to be perfectly joined together in the same mind and judgment, you will be setting your family up for success in this world and the next.

Let's Pray

Dear Heavenly Father…I thank You for this family that You've blessed me with. I pray that You would help me to set the correct vision and lead them in the right way…the way that You have determined that they need to go. Help harmony to reign in our household, and that we would all strive to be within Your will. Thank You in advance for the joys we will experience as we strive together for the kingdom. Amen.

THE FAMILY DYNAMIC

"And let us consider how to stir up one another to love and good works, not neglecting to meet together, as is the habit of some, but encouraging one another, and all the more as you see the day drawing near. " –Hebrews 10:24-25 (ESV)

When I first thought about the family dynamic, I related it to the standard individual parts of a family. There's dad, mom, brother, sister and the occasional family pet. Next, I related those parts to standard traditional roles. You know, dad goes to work. Mom cooks and takes care of the kids. The kids behave and get good grades in school. Sparky the dog, plays fetch and never has an accident on the rug. But as I unwrapped the family dynamic just a little further, I discovered that the family dynamic is more involved than just basic parts and roles.

One definition of the word dynamic is; "a force that stimulates change or progress to a system or process." With this definition in mind, family dynamic has more to do with progressing together than with who is doing what chore on which particular day.

I like to think practically. I had to define family dynamic in practical terms for my own sake. So, if my role is to cook dinner, practically speaking, what change or progress does me making dinner stir up? Does the meal I serve progress the family toward good health or poor health? Do I exhibit a force that stimulates change when I serve a healthy meal, meet together at the table, and speak encouragement with my family? This is a practical side of Hebrews 10:24-25.

Along the same line of thought, do my husband's extra hours at work stimulate the positive change needed inside the family? Do my kids exhibit more sibling comradery or sibling rivalry when they interact? These small everyday occurrences influence how my family moves.

Lastly, I had to ask myself, how is my family progressing? I want my family to move together in the direction of God. Each member of the family must understand that they impact the family as a whole and not just themselves. Christ is about our individual salvation, but He is also the God of the collective souls. Christ loves the church family and the families that make up the church. Christ met together with his church family and Christ loved to eat dinner with individual families every chance He could during His time here on earth. It's important that my family understands that the road to Heaven is a lot easier to walk as a family, influencing and encouraging each other to finish the race. What about you, how is your family progressing? Is your family progressing the way God said in Hebrews 10: 24-25?

To help family members understand their force on the family, meet together often and talk about it. Talk about what God says about allowing our actions to move the family toward love and good works. Make certain through consistent prayer, the reading of God's word, and meeting together as a family, that the family is progressing toward God. The end result of this kind of family dynamic is a Dynamic Family!

Let's Pray

Dear Lord, I want my family to progress towards you. I, want to progress towards you. I ask Jesus that you impact my heart and fill me with encouragement so that I can be a positive impact on my family. In Jesus' name, Amen.

THE FAMILY IDENTITY

"Hello! My name is Clinton Lindo; I'm a database administrator. Nice to meet you!" I've lost count of how many times I've said those words. And you've probably said something very similar to this; declaring your name and what you do to a complete stranger. Why do we do this? I believe we are defining ourselves in the eyes of the person we are talking to; we are identifying ourselves. Greeting people like this is a standard-level greeting; it makes sense that we state what our name is, but why do we pair it to our occupation? I believe that we are conditioned to think of our occupation as the most important aspect that defines us outside of our names. Society looks at our jobs, what we do for a living, as the most important aspect of our existence.

That made sense to me until I heard these words: "Hi, I'm Dr. Laura and I am my kids' mom." Some people may recognize those well-known words as belonging to Dr. Laura Schlesinger, a popular syndicated radio host. Despite being a radio host, an author, and a doctor, her greeting defined herself as the mother to her children. This was what she considered the most important aspect and therefore how she wished to be identified. This made me think; when I identify myself as a database administrator, what am I telling people? Am I in a way telling people that the job that I do is the most important aspect of my life and that's what I want people to know? Is that something that I truly believe? This may be something that we have to address within ourselves. What part of our existence trumps all others when it comes to priorities and decision making? Is it our gifts or talents? Is it our denomination? What is it for you?

This approach applies to families as well. No, when we introduce our family, we don't say, "Hi, we're the Lindo's, and we are writers." It is not a usual greeting; we don't usually have an identity for our families. But…might we need to reconsider that? Not necessarily regarding greeting strangers, but how we consider our priorities and decision-making. That identity can be simple; for example, "We are Smiths and Smiths do not swear." It can be a little more important; in my family, I've said to our children, "We are Lindo's and Lindo's don't misuse credit cards." It also might be something that is very important: "We are Smiths and Smiths believe in Christian education." Principles that are important to the family help define or identify the family and are considered first when making difficult decisions.

As the father, you should decide what principles and direction identify your family. No, not all by yourself; your wife is your helpmeet; she needs to help in determining those principles and direction. Getting her fully on-board is important because, in many family settings, she will be spending more time nurturing the children and if she is fully onboard, she will make sure the children know what those principles and directions are. Also, once the family identity is selected, this is not for the children only; it's for the whole family. This is not a "do as I say, not as I do" situation. If you're a Smith, and Smiths do not swear, swearing when your team's receiver drops a crucial pass late in an important game is unacceptable. Children will see how important these principles are and will most likely incorporate them once they have their own family.

This definitely applies to spiritual things as well. Abraham, a strong fatherly example in most of what he did, understood the importance of these things. God said of Abraham in **Genesis 18:19, "I have singled him out so that he will direct his sons and their families to keep the way of the Lord by doing what is right and just. Then I will do for Abraham all that I have promised." (NLT)** We should be no different than Abraham in this example. And hopefully, the main thing that your family will use to identify themselves will be, "We are the Smiths, and the Smiths are going to the Kingdom." We need to maintain a heavenly mindset in our families at all times and actively work toward getting caught up in the air once Christ breaks through the clouds of glory. All decisions, family-based or otherwise, need to be made with this as a priority and the ultimate goal. As the father, you need to keep the vision of presenting your family to the Savior in the center of your mind. No aspect of you or your family's identity is more important than that.

Let's Pray

Lord, I ask You to help me to set the right direction and definition of our family. Help me to hear where You want our family to go…what You want our family to do. Help us to have the identity that You have set for us. And Lord, help us to be focused on making it into the kingdom where we can praise you together as a family. Amen.

THE FAMILY IDENTITY

"So God created mankind in his own image, in the image of God he created them; male and female he created them." –Genesis 1:27 (ESV)

I have a blended family. I have two wonderful boys of my own and a third wonderful, younger boy with my wonderful husband, Clinton Lindo. My two older boys still carry my ex-husband's last name, Are'.

One day, my family and I were about to leave a gathering at a friend's house. To get my scattered boys together, I yelled, "the Lindo and Are' family is about to leave!" The boys came running and we were set to go. However, one of the Elders from my church, a very kind and wise man, asked if he could talk to me aside for a moment. Privately, he gave me one of the worse reprimands I've ever had!

He explained the disservice I was doing to my husband and the boys by identifying them as two households instead of one. He said my family was one unit under the headship of Clinton Lindo. Yes, my two boys have a different last name, but they were living under, being provided for, and being loved by the man named Lindo. It is by the Lindo name that all of us are identified. At church, at school, in public, we are called the Lindo family. I thanked my Elder, nursed my feelings from the spiritual spanking, and yelled my closing statement before leaving," All of the Lindo household, let's go!"

Got it, we are the Lindo's. That means something. We even have family meetings about what the Lindo name means and how the Lindo's are to behave. This does not take away from the boys Are' family ties, but the Elder was right. Albeit two names, our family is one family. We identify as The Lindo Family.

Okay, but what does that really mean for my identity? Is taking my husband's last name, or being my children's mother, all to my identity in the family? It's true that I function as part of the Lindo household, but I am my own person too. Right?

The answer to this question for me was found in the first book of the Bible, **Genesis 1:27. "So God created mankind in his own image, in the image of God he created them; male and female he created them."**

I am individually created in the image of God. I reflect who He is. How I function in the Lindo household should reflect how God functions. My words are a reflection of His words. My attitude is a reflection of His attitude. My actions are a reflection of His actions.

When I act as a reflection of God in my home, my personal identity in the family becomes very clear. As I reflect God's heart, I become the Heart of my home. I am a conduit that allows God to supply me with love so that I can supply my family with love. Just as my first two boys have an individual last name and are part of the bigger family, I have an individual function within my bigger family. But it is still one family, with one family identity.

To sum up my family identity: I am a Lindo. I am a wife and mother. I am God's heart in my home. I am a reflection of God. I am made in the image of God.

What is your family's identity? Particularly, what is your individual, God-given, identity within your family? If you are not sure. Read Genesis 1:27.

Let's Pray

Heavenly Father, thank you for creating me in your image, with my very own identity. Help me to function in my bigger family without losing who you made me to be. Help me to always reflect Your heart. In Jesus' name, Amen.

THE FAMILY RELATIONSHIP WITH CHRIST

What comes to mind when you hear the words "a good relationship"? You might think of a couple that laughs together, holds hands, finishes each other's sentences, and genuinely loves to be around each other. I have this type of relationship with my wife, and it is as awesome as it sounds. We laugh at our private jokes, have long conversations, love spending time together, and usually can't wait until we're together again when we're apart. We've had people describe us as having a "good relationship" and I definitely cannot disagree. How we act together didn't happen overnight, though. We spent a lot of time together, before and after we got married. We would talk for hours in person and on the phone. We set time aside for each other, prioritizing our time together above other things, sometimes even over sleep. We didn't only have quantity time, but quality time.

As good as we are together, I doubt we are unique. If I were to ask you about how you and your wife got together, I'm sure we'd end up talking about long phone conversations, laughing together, sometimes at silly things, lots of great dates and just having fun. I'm nearly positive you prioritized and rearranged your time so that you could have as much time as possible with her; you looked forward to it.

So, the question is, when we talk about a relationship with Christ, why do some of us believe it's different? Some of us might believe that a good relationship with Christ can be maintained through occasional attendance at weekly church services and only praying when there's a problem that we tried to resolve ourselves and were unsuccessful. If we were to equate that to a human relationship, how would you feel if your then-girlfriend occasionally saw you when it suited her, hardly called you, and when she did, she always needed something? Would someone, or would you, describe that as a good relationship?

A good relationship with Christ includes quantity time. This would look like attending regular church services, having daily devotion and prayer, carving out an amount of time that belongs only to the Lord. A good relationship with Christ includes quality time. The time we spend with the Lord should be meaningful, not just an amount of time where we're constantly checking our watch (or phone) to see when that time will end. A good relationship with Christ is prioritized. Time with the Savior is not always immediately usurped by something else deemed more important. After all, **Deuteronomy 16:5 says, "And you must love the Lord your God with all your heart, all your soul, and all your strength." (NLT)**

As the father, the priest of the home, our relationship with Christ will carry over to the rest of the household. Sending our family to church and not going ourselves is unacceptable. Our children will look at church as just an obligation that needs to be filled and will not see its importance. Just like how our sons will mold how they treat their future wives by watching how we treat our wives, our children will mold how they approach the Lord by watching what importance we give to the relationship. Our children will ultimately follow our example more than they will follow our directive.

A family relationship with Christ looks like having family worship regularly, having family prayer, attending church regularly, even getting involved in events and church offices if possible. And doing all of this with enthusiasm so that our children pick up on how important it is. You might be lacking that enthusiasm, but that's okay. It's not like God does not know you are less than enthused with putting in this effort. Talk to him; that's what He's there for. Be honest, talk to Him about where you are, and ask for a new heart, one that turns toward Him easily. Christ said that he'd take our heart of stone out of our flesh and give us a heart of flesh. Then, ask Him to direct you in directing your family. Believe me; this is what He's waiting for and will be more than happy to inspire you with ideas to get the family pointed in the right direction.

Let's Pray

Dear heavenly Father, I am sorry for the times that I've neglected You, and didn't think it important to spend time with You. I ask that You help me with that right now. Help my relationship with You to be deep and meaningful. And then help me to convey that same sentiment to the family You've blessed me with. Help us all to love You with all our heart, all our soul and all our strength. In Jesus' name, Amen.

THE FAMILY RELATIONSHIP WITH CHRIST

In my home, an individual relationship with Christ is repeatedly encouraged through bible reading, prayer, and example. After all, a relationship with Christ is the most vital relationship a person can have.

Also, in my home, the importance of a relationship with each other is conveyed over and over again through prayer, family meetings, and family time together.

But I realized there was a relationship piece missing. Individual, personal relationship to Christ, check. Respectful relationships to each other in the family, check. But what about the family relationship to Christ? What is the collective family relationship to Christ?

I've poured through articles and writings about the family relationship to each other. I've read quotes that say things like, "The Family that prays together stays together", and "In time of test, family is best." I've read books about how to get along with your children and the importance of children obeying their parents—all great information on relationships within the family. But what I was searching for was information about my family's relationship as a whole with Christ.

I found the answer I needed in **Romans 12:4-8, 21, "⁴ For as we have many members in one body, and all members have not the same office: ⁵ So we, being many, are one body in Christ, and every one members one of another. ⁶ Having then gifts differing according to the grace that is given to us, whether prophecy, let us prophesy according to the proportion of faith; ⁷ Or ministry, let us wait on our ministering: or he that teacheth, on teaching; ⁸ Or he that exhorteth, on exhortation: he that giveth, let him do it with simplicity; he that ruleth, with diligence; he that sheweth mercy, with cheerfulness. ²¹ Be not overcome of evil, but overcome evil with good." (KJV)**

I've heard numerous pastors use this verse when addressing their church congregation to encourage unity and the spirit of working together as a whole church. As I thought about this verse, I realized that a church congregation at large is simply a collection of smaller congregations, smaller churches, if you will. In other words, the larger church congregation is made up of smaller family-sized churches.

Using this rationale, I understood that my family is a church, and my home is my children's first church experience. I was confident in running my physical home, cooking, cleaning, kissing boo-boos. But then questions came flooding in:

- Was I running my home-church with the same confidence?

- Am I teaching my family the principles of being one body in Christ?

- Am I teaching them about their spiritual gifts and allowing them to use them in my home?

- Are they helping each other overcome evil by doing good in my home?

- Is my home-church a Romans 12 church?

There was no way I could answer yes to all my questions, but I constantly pray that Christ will turn our home-church into the type of home-church He is coming back for.

Revelation 19:7-8 says, "Let us be glad and rejoice and give Him glory, for the marriage of the Lamb has come, and His wife has made herself ready. And to her it was granted to be arrayed in fine linen, clean and bright, for the fine linen is the righteous acts of the saints." (NKJV) The bible tells us that Christ is coming for his bride, the church. Not the huge congregational church, but the family-sized church, his young bride, the Romans 12 church. This is the family relationship to Christ. My family, your family is His precious bride.

Let's Pray

Dear Jesus, one day soon you will come back for your people, your bride. Help our home be a place that works together to overcome evil with good. When you return, may our little home-church be ready to go with you to the place you have prepared for us in Heaven. In Jesus' name, Amen.

THE FAMILY PURPOSE

I've always been fascinated by astronomy. I love reading about planets and galaxies, and I especially love reading about how intricately everything works together. I'm amazed at how big the earth is, then how small it is compared to the sun, and how small the sun is compared to much bigger stars...this can go on and on and on. It is very easy to look at all of that, compare ourselves to it and ask the question, why am I here and what purpose do I even serve? I've seen people get depressed over the feeling of insignificance they get with comparing themselves to the cosmos, their lifespan to eternity.

Being a Christian, we should never need to experience this existential crisis. We might feel insignificant when comparing ourselves to the universe, but that is not how God sees us. Looking at the universe will always bring me back to the

Lord; everything in the universe is a testament to his orchestrating power. When we start to explore how big the universe is, we are reminded of how big and powerful our God really is. Yet, even though our God is omnipotent, omniscient, omnipresent, and probably a bunch of other omnis, He still came down to this earth, took on human form and died for *us*. Not only did He sacrifice His life, but you can also, right this second, speak to Him, and He will hear you. You are vitally important to the Lord. These thoughts should make any feelings of insignificance completely disappear.

So, what is our purpose? We should define our purpose in the context of what God wants from us. He wants us to be a living testimony to his saving power; that's not only speaking to others about all of the different ways God has come through for you, opened doors for you or spared your life. It's also orienting our lives to reflect His goodness better so that when people look at our lives, they will want what we have. We are also supposed to be Christ's body, to be His hands and feet so that we can reach and help the people Christ loves. **Ephesians 2:10 says, "For we are His workmanship, created in Christ Jesus for good works, which God prepared beforehand that we should walk in them." (NKJV)**

What is our purpose as fathers? Keeping in mind our general purpose, our jobs as fathers are to reflect God to our families, to direct them to the Lord, and regularly bring them before the throne of grace. Our children's view of God will be carbon copies of how we view Him, so we need to have a sincere and personal relationship with God ourselves so we can impart that to our families. This may seem to be a pretty hefty responsibility, and it is. However, God did not intend us to do this without any help; He stands ready and able to assist you whenever you feel you are falling short.

That brings us to our family's purpose, which should be similar to our individual purposes; to be a living testimony and operate as Christ's body. How does your family do that? That's not a question that this devotion can answer. Each of us and each of our families are given specific talents that would be used to help us navigate this life and further God's kingdom. We need to convene our families and talk about what the family members' gifts and talents are. If the children are young, and there is a talent that seems to be manifesting in them, cultivate it; point them in specific directions that would help them develop that talent. Then talk about how that talent can help them and help God. Sometimes, those talents will work together with other family members; sometimes, it might be more of a solo thing. In any case, pray about your family's purpose; ask God for strength, wisdom and consistency as you point your family toward a future of discovering your talents and using them for yourselves and the Lord. The road you take will be a very rewarding one.

Let's Pray

Lord, first, thank You for loving us enough to die for us. Thank You for showing us that love every single day. Help me to reflect that same love to my family and help us all to show that love to others. As we go out into the world, help others to see You in what we say and in what we do. Help us to love them just like you love us. In Jesus' name, amen.

THE FAMILY PURPOSE

It seemed that it was always easy for me to see the purpose of others than to see my own purpose. And even more so with other families. I saw the Smith family work together in health ministry and I was envious because they had a purpose. I wasn't jealous of them in a bad way, but I was envious that they were working together in service. Then I watched as the Jones family sang gospel music together, ministering in song, and again I was envious. It seemed as though all the families around me had a purpose. They were all working together—all except mine.

So, I prayed about it and found this scripture, **1 Peter 2:9, "But you are a chosen people, a royal priesthood, a holy nation, God's special possession, that you may declare the praises of him who called**

**you out of darkness into his wonderful light."
(NIV)**

I thought to myself, oh, this is easy, just praise the Lord all the time! Declare His praises! My family and I could do that. Then, I re-read the verse and discovered there was just a little more to it. There was just a little more to family purpose than just praising the Lord all the time.

The scripture says to "declare the praises of him who called you out of darkness into his wonderful light." If my family is to declare the praises of the Lord, we cannot do this in a place of darkness. Don't get me wrong, we can praise the Lord in troubled times, in times of despair, but the dark place this verse refers to is a place of the lack of knowledge of the Lord. Peter tells us that when we accept Christ, we are no longer in darkness. We now walk in His wonderful light. We have a new life, and in that new life, we are God's special possession. This acceptance, this new life where God's hand snatches us from darkness into light is the praise we have to declare.

Through this verse, God helped me understand that the purpose of the family is to do its best to ensure that each member of the family moves from darkness into light. As each member moves, God's praises are declared. The family purpose is to encourage the acceptance of Christ within the family and then declare His praises for what He has done.

Understand that there is an enemy that will do all he can to keep the family in darkness. He will do all he can to keep family members from accepting the Light and new life in Christ. This is when the family should declare God's praises all the more. Keep praying for each family member. Keep telling the story of how He brought other members from darkness to light. Pray together often as a family.

It may take some time, but never quit until your family becomes that Holy nation, that royal priesthood, that chosen people Peter spoke about. This is the family purpose; to leave the darkness and come to the Light, then declare the praises of the Lord who chose you and brought you out.

My family may not minister the same way the Smith family ministers or sing like the Jones family sings, but when the Lindo Family prays for each other, when the Lindo family intercedes for each other, when the Lindo family comforts and cares for each other, when the Lindo family declares the goodness and salvation of God within the family, we are in our purpose. How about your family? God has a purpose for your family as well. Pray and talk to God about your family's purpose. It's a prayer God is looking forward to receiving and answering.

Let's Pray

Heavenly Father, help us to fulfill our purpose as a family. Help us to care about each other's salvation so that no one is walking in darkness but are bathed in Your precious light. You, Lord, are worthy of all of our praise. In Jesus' name, Amen.

Theme 2 – Construction and Repair

When a home is being constructed, any issues and problems must be addressed as soon as they are discovered. If they are ignored, and construction continues, the integrity of the home would be at risk, and the longer they are ignored, the harder they are to remedy. Every family walks through hard times together, and sometimes those circumstances are out of our control. This section of the devotional addresses some common issues and will aid you in starting to repair any damage. The topics addressed in this section are Family Feelings, Family Drama, Family Conflict, Family Loss, Family Pride and Family Forgiveness.

FAMILY FEELINGS

When I was growing up and I got upset over something my parents were saying to me, my demeanor would come out in my voice. That's when I heard the statement that maybe quite a few of us have heard before, "You need to change your tone right now." My father would say, "You need to take that bass out of your voice." I would alter my voice pretty quickly because the next parental correction was not guaranteed to be verbal. I realize now that my parents were giving me a crash course on controlling my feelings.

This was not about changing how I felt but changing how what I was feeling impacted my actions. In this particular case, it was how what I was feeling came out in my voice. My parents clearly felt that controlling my voice was possible regardless of how I felt. Our heavenly Father backs this sentiment up in the first part of **Ephesians 4:26 which says, "Be angry, and do not sin." (NKJV)** Here, God is giving us license to be angry. He made us with these emotions, so He expects us to be annoyed sometimes, irate sometimes, and downright incensed sometimes. However, He tells us that being angry does not need to lead to sin, meaning we can control how our anger governs our actions.

Some people might say, "I can't control myself when I'm mad; I'm acting out of anger and people have to understand that." First, it is untrue that we can't control ourselves when we're angry. There is something called the "Phone Call Test." When someone is angry, shouting all sorts of hateful and horrible things, what if the phone rings and there's a best friend on the other end, or maybe an old college roommate you haven't heard from in forever? That anger quickly dissipates and suddenly the voice comes down to a regular volume and there might even be some laughs during that conversation. That should inform them that, yes, they can control what they do when they are angry if they are motivated to do so. What these people are saying is that they don't *want* to control themselves when they are angry. Second, after the moment has passed, saying that "the anger made me say it" does not take away the hurt and pain of the things said in anger. That hurt and pain will linger long after the argument is done.

As fathers, we need to make sure that our children understand that the way they are feeling does not need to and shouldn't govern our actions. Even though they get angry or upset, they need to know that their actions need to be measured and controlled. We can sympathize with them, telling them we understand why they are angry; however, they should also understand that whatever they are feeling offers no excuse for anything they might do. Children that don't learn to untether their actions from their feelings will grow up to be adults who might need to be corrected much more harshly than they would have at home.

How we act needn't be focused on just negative feelings, but positive as well. At those times, I believe we need to express ourselves, especially if we're feeling happiness toward another member of the household. Tell them how you feel; this is particularly for us men who tend to like to keep our feelings bottled up. Taking the time to express ourselves, especially to our spouses, will definitely make our wives happier and will also increase their feelings of security. If you want to see your wife glow, tell her that the last meal she made was great and it just made you love her even more.

Whether we are dealing with negative feelings or positive feelings, take them both to the Lord. For the negative feelings, we need to be asking Him to help us deal with the feelings of anger or sadness that we are experiencing and asking Him for help with self-control. We need to go to the Lord in thanksgiving for the positive feelings. We need to have an attitude of gratitude with God and thank Him for all the good things taking place in our lives. Regardless of how we are feeling, speaking to the Lord will always make things even better; He is the one that created us with these feelings, He'll know what we ought to be doing.

Let's Pray

Lord, I know I can get upset sometimes, but I ask You to give me complete reign over my actions. When I get angry, help me to think before I act…to think before I talk. Give me the strength to bring any negative feelings to You and also help me to thank You when I am feeling good. Help me to lead my family by example when controlling my reactions, and help me to teach them to go to You for help. In Jesus' name, amen.

FAMILY FEELINGS

"Always be humble and gentle. Be patient with each other, making allowance for each other's faults because of your love." –Ephesians 4:2 (NLT)

I know that it's stereotypical to believe that girls display more of an array of feelings than boys, but as a mom of three boys, I watched my boys express or exhibit every definable feeling there is. Feelings like anxiety, anger, bashfulness, delight, depression, joy, sadness, and a host of other feelings from A-Z.

One thing I recognize is that each feeling they unveil is *their* feeling. It belongs to them. I cannot dictate what my sons, or for that matter what my husband, feels. When my boys were young, I would try and help them verbalize their feelings. I would correct and reward how they manifested their feelings. In other words, although they were entitled to all their feelings, they were not entitled to all behaviors. Now that they are adults, I simply try to respect their feelings. Yet still, the behaviors stemming from these feelings must be guided in my boys, my husband, and me. Yes, my own feeling-behaviors need to be checked!

To do this, I had to reconcile something first. I know that the bible says that feelings cannot be trusted; they can be deceitful. (**Proverbs 28:26 "26 He that trusteth in his own heart is a fool: but whoso walketh wisely, he shall be delivered." KJV**) So, this means I should never pay attention to my feelings? But on the other hand, I know that God has equipped me with certain feelings that help me provide good counsel to my husband. (**Genesis 2:18 "18 Now the Lord God said, "It is not good (beneficial) for the man to be alone; I will make him a helper [one who balances him—a counterpart who is] [a]suitable and complementary for him." AMP**) So, this means I should pay attention to my feelings? Pay attention or don't pay attention, well, which is it? After all, the bible does not contradict itself, so this has to make sense somehow.

The reason the bible is not contradictory here is that there are two types of feelings, human and Godly. Human feelings are those survival, instinctive, gut feelings we have. Everyone has them; they are not particular to gender. Men and women, and children have "gut" feelings. Dad feels like that job opportunity comes with hidden strings. Mom feels like the new neighbors might be nice people to associate with. Little Johnny feels like that kid who wants to play might be mean. Human feelings have their place, but they can also be very wrong. Like the bible tells us, they can fail.

Godly feelings work differently. These feelings are Holy Spirit connected. The dictionary defines them as: "The ability to understand something immediately, without the need for conscious reasoning." Sometimes this is referred to as intuition, but calling it intuition is insufficient. Godly feelings are high above intuition. These feelings are unflawed and come from a source outside of yourself. Almost like understanding a language you never studied, the Holy Spirit touches your senses, and you just know. These Godly feelings are also not particular to gender; men and women have them. Children can have Godly feelings as well. The Holy Spirit touches little ones too!

When we consider feelings, we must consider the source of those feelings. Are they human feelings? If they are human feelings, are they connected to a behavior that should be rewarded or corrected? Are they Godly feelings that need to be heard, prayed about, and acted upon?

Feelings and behaviors are a part of each family because they are a part of each person in the family. Managing them well within the family is no small feat, but they can be managed.

Let Us Pray

Our Father, You said we are fearfully and wonderfully made. Help us to manage our feelings and behaviors. Help us to hear the Holy Spirit as He reaches for our hearts. Please grant our family patience and love toward each other. In Jesus' name, Amen.

FAMILY DRAMA

I wish we could say that once we declare our home to be a Christian home, that the home will no longer have any problems. From that point on, everything will be rainbows and flowers (for the ladies) and shade trees and freshly-cut grass (for the men). Unfortunately, Christ did not promise us a perfect time on earth, and therefore we are bound to run into problems in our homes. Some of those problems might be considered more intense than others, or what some people might refer to as drama.

I know that the word drama sparks thoughts of cheesy soap operas with mournful music and dramatic close-ups at emotionally fraught moments. That might make us feel that drama, especially from a man's perspective, is childish and pointless, and the less time devoted to it, the better. Unfortunately, just like some of these soap operas that feel like they've been broadcast since the inception of television, some drama doesn't just go away. This is because drama is based on our feelings toward a person or situation, and emotions have a way of getting under our skin and staying there.

Acknowledging that drama is something that we need to address, there should be some ground rules in place. The number one ground rule is this: what happens in the family, stays in the family. Any problems that we have with our wives or that our children have with each other, stays within the four (or more) walls of your house. This needs to be drilled into our children at an early enough age; that it's second nature to keep family secrets away from outsiders. This is not to keep from bringing a problem to a counselor or pastor if the problem requires it; I encourage seeking help if need be. This is more about trying to keep from telling a family story to friends as a joke or using it as a way to bring down a family member. This outside confidant will more likely than not bring up those problems repeatedly, and that serves to keep the problem from fading. Stories also have a nasty habit of not staying put with who we tell them to, and there's nothing worse than hearing about your failings from some acquaintance that you hardly know. This is a huge barrier to forgiving and forgetting the problem.

Another important ground rule is that no matter our issues with our family member(s), we are still a family and are still protective of each other. If you overheard me having a disagreement with my wife and later came to me badmouthing her based on what you heard, I guarantee that your day would go downhill from there. No matter what we might be going through at any particular moment, it doesn't change the fact that my wife is an integral part of my life and I love her more than I do myself. It is important to instill a sense of family loyalty and advocacy that takes over once a family member interacts with anyone outside of the family circle and we should feel a righteous sense of protection arise within us when one of the family is spoken about in less than glowing terms.

Lastly, allow drama to fade once resolved. Most drama will be a source of embarrassment for one or more family members, so constantly bringing it up to get a chuckle out of guests (or to assert one's superiority) will prolong the discomfort associated with the drama. That family member may even say that bringing it up is fine and smile through gritted teeth when everyone's laughing at their expense. This is the way one shows that the drama is done with; by leaving it in the past. Even if they are the ones to bring it up, let them do so; it is their story to tell. This allows each family member to feel safe within the family and allows children to share more of what's going on with them when they see how protective the family is of each other.

Drama is incredibly difficult to avoid. Since we are all different people, it is bound to rear its ugly head; the enemy will make sure of it. **Ephesians 4:2-3 says, "With all lowliness and gentleness, with**

longsuffering, bearing with one another in love, endeavoring to keep the unity of the Spirit in the bond of peace." (NKJV) We need to make sure that we are striving for that unity of the Spirit in our homes; it should be our overall goal. Our job as family members, and especially as fathers, is to make sure that when drama knocks on your family's door, that it will be a very short visit.

Let's Pray

Dear heavenly Father, I ask You to give me wisdom and insight as I deal with drama that arises in my family. Give me the right words to say to help defuse situations, and also guide my actions so that drama is short-lived. I thank you in advance for helping us to maintain peace and harmony in our household. In Jesus' name, amen.

FAMILY DRAMA

"Love is patient and kind. Love is not jealous or boastful or proud or rude. It does not demand its own way. It is not irritable, and it keeps no record of being wronged." –1 Corinthians 13:4-5 (NLT)

Ladies and gentlemen, we present to you the winner of the Ms. Drama Queen pageant (drum roll please), me! I admit it; I can be sort of a Drama Queen! I also know that I am not the only reigning mom wearing a drama queen crown.

Are you a Ms. Drama Queen too? Not sure? Well, there is an easy way to expose the dramatic diva in us. Just open your bible and stand in front of the drama queen detector mirror found in 1 Corinthians 13:4-5, and take a look at yourself on any given day.

This Corinthian mirror tells me to be patient and kind. Was I patient when I told my kids that they "never come when I call," after they came a few seconds later than I wanted them to? Was I patient when I yelled at my husband for not yelling at the kids for playing in the living room? Was I kind when I told my son, "Serves you right," when he tripped on his shoelace after I told him to tie it? Nope. Instead, I was pretty dramatic in my responses. Drama Queen detected.

According to my Corinthian mirror, I should not demand my own way. Was I demanding my own way when my husband and children wanted to leave the church to go home but had to wait until I finished chit-chatting with my friends? Was I demanding my own way when I expected my children to clean their rooms, with lightning speed, to a standard that I don't even maintain in my own room? The short answer, yes. Drama Queen detected.

God's word says, I should not be irritable nor should I keep a record of being wronged. How many times have I pushed my boys and my husband away because I was in a bad mood? How many times have I reminded my children and my husband of the things they forgot or neglected to do when I asked? The answer is too many times. If the drama queen detector mirror came with an alarm and pointer arrow, it would definitely sound off and point to me, mom the Drama Queen.

But the great thing about God's word is that its verses can detect a problem and the same verses can fix the problem. When my drama queen wants to rear up her out-of-control head, I remember that I love my family, and then I remember what 1 Corinthians 13 tells me love is. Love is patient and kind. I remember that my family needs their wife and mom; they don't need a drama queen.

There will be lots of dramatic episodes in any family, especially with all of the different personalities running around under the same roof. In fact, it may feel like there is never a drama-free day. Keep 1 Corinthians 13 handy, pin it up on your wall and read it aloud each morning. By reading this each day, it will help ensure the loving wife and mom in us is part of the cast in every family episode. Drama Queens might make for good television, but they don't belong on our family stage or in the Heavenly arena.

Let's Pray

Dear Jesus, this world offers enough drama. As I look to you to be a calming, peaceful voice in my spirit, help me to bring calm and peacefulness to my family. Let patience rein in my home instead of drama. In Jesus' name, Amen.

FAMILY CONFLICT

"All is fair in love and war" is a pretty well-known statement. What is funny about it is just how false it is. Very few people would ever consider everything to be fair when it comes to love. Even when it comes to war, where two or more sides are attempting to kill as many members of the opposing side as possible, they are supposed to abide by rules set by the Geneva Convention. Looking at a much smaller conflict, like boxing or MMA fighting, there are set rules regarding where you can hit your opponent and when.

As the above example in war and in professional fighting shows, there are rules to conflict. And as much as we try, it will be nearly impossible to avoid conflict in our families, so when we experience conflict in our homes, there should be rules associated with that conflict.

To start with, we don't like the word "fight" in our household and lean more toward the term "conflict resolution." This points us toward the first important rule to conflict: the purpose of the conflict should be to resolve the conflict, not to hurt someone else. The purpose of a "fight" is to hurt the other person as much as possible so as to render them unwilling or unable to fight any longer. The purpose of a "conflict resolution" is to resolve the problem and nothing more. Even if the conflict started off with the best intentions, it is not difficult to find ourselves devolving into personal attacks if the conflict resolution is not going our way. If we try to win a fight by emotionally harming our opponent so much that they no longer want to fight, we might have achieved a meaningless, hollow victory, but the conflict will still remain unresolved. In fact, we might have now ensured that there are two conflicts to resolve now.

Another rule of conflict resolution is that one person speaks, the other or others listen. More than one person trying to speak at the same time means that nobody gets heard, and when people don't get heard, they tend to raise their voices. This will almost always transform into shouting matches, and when people are screaming at each other, listening is at a minimum, and problems rarely get resolved. Take turns talking, taking the time to thoughtfully listen to the other person's argument and respond to what they said, not to what you think they meant. Leave the shouting and screaming for watching sports and exciting movies.

If it is clear that the conflict will be resolved in a way other than what we want, this is not the time to bring up older arguments where we were in the right. Acting in this way only serves to feed our ego, no more, and there's no place for that in a conflict resolution. And I hope we don't need to be told that conflict resolution should never ever be physical unless by physical, we mean a reassuring hug when it is all over.

As fathers, we need to teach by example as well as by word. Children who grow up in households where their parents never raise their voices or hands to each other become adults who don't raise their voices or their hands to their spouses. This also extends to how we address our children. Something they've done may have angered us; however, we should try to speak to them in measured tones, explaining to them why what they did upset us, as well as the consequences of their actions.

It is clear that Christ wanted us to have this approach to conflict resolution when He said **in Matthew 5:9, "Blessed are the peacemakers, For they shall be called sons of God." (NKJV)** He wanted to specifically commend people whose goal was to make peace; these are the people that will help make the world a better place. Having this focus on fighting or conflict resolution is not easy if one is used to doing things another way. Changing a habit is not the easiest thing to do. Take it to the Lord, and ask Him to make your household into a

quieter and gentler place. Your family will thank
you for it.

Let's Pray

Dear Father in heaven, I understand that there will be disagreements in the family you have gifted us. I ask that you would help us to resolve those agreements without violence, without yelling, without name-calling and without resentment toward one another afterward. Help that each conflict resolution will bring us closer to each other as a family and closer to You. Thank you, and in Jesus' name, amen.

FAMILY CONFLICT

"Let each of you look not only to his own interests, but also to the interests of others." **–Philippians 2:4 (ESV)**

Growing up, my brother and I were typical little kids. He had his room and I had mine. He had his action figures, and I had my dolls. We got along okay and had some fun together. My brother is five years older than me, so we didn't have a whole lot in common, but we would get together sometimes to sneakily plot against mom for a snack or try and manipulate dad to bring us our favorite candy from the store. The two of us were pretty convincing together. He was the mastermind behind the planning and would tell me what to ask for. I was the adorable one with the big brown eyes who would sweetly execute the diabolical plan. That's how my brother and I looked out for each other.

Things dramatically changed between us when I was 9 years old. My parents got divorced and my dad moved seven states away. Back then, I didn't have the understanding to verbalize what was happening between my brother and me. What I understand now is that the divorce threw the two of us into a constant state of conflict.

Conflict among siblings is nothing new, of course. We read in the bible about two brothers, twins Jacob and Esau, who took no care for the interest of each other and only cared about themselves. Their selfish interest led to the thievery of a birthright and a grudge of revenge. (Read Genesis 27.)

Things were so different for my brother and I in this new divorced world order. Prior to the divorce, if my brother was busy with my mom, I could just go and hang out with my dad. Now there was only one parent, mom, and we constantly jockeyed for position with her. To make matters worse, with mom working extra hours to make ends meet, her free time was very limited. In this divorced world, we battled over the tv, a seat in the car, snacks, stuff we had never battled over before. Everything quickly became me vs him, my interests vs his interests. Instead of plotting together, we plotted against each other. As the years went by, we grew emotionally apart and then physically apart when he moved to another state. I missed my brother, but honestly, I didn't miss all the conflict.

Later as life would have it, my brother moved back to my home state and we were able to connect again. I was afraid our conflict-ridden attitudes had followed us into our adulthood. That's the saddest thing about family conflict; it will grow and permanently take up residence if allowed.

But praise God for the lessons in Philippians 2:4, "Let each of you look not only to his own interests, but also to the interests of others." Currently, my brother looks after our aging mother, and I care for our aging father. Caring for parents is an honor but not always easy, so we look out for each other. His interests are mine, and mine are his. We plan and strategize on how to best handle our parents together. We disagree sometimes, but there is no room for conflict. We recognize that we need each other. Oh, how I wish we had discovered this bible gem sooner. Those twins, Jacob and Esau were able to reconcile many years later, but like my brother and me, so much time we could have been connected was wasted, time that we cannot recover.

My hope is that every family learns the power of this friendship saving, conflict conquering verse. Teach this to your children early; repeat it in your worships and family meetings. Allow these words that Christ imparted to us to change your house of conflict to a house of peace and togetherness.

Let's Pray

Dear Jesus, You did not create us to be in rounds of conflict. You placed man in a perfect garden until sin entered and nothing since has been the same. Lord, please

*keep my home a place of peace and reconciliation until
You come to take us to our home where all conflict will
end. In Jesus' name, Amen.*

FAMILY LOSS

Not too long ago, I read a story about a tween girl, 12 or 13-years-old, who fell deeply in love with her boyfriend. I already hear your thoughts; deeply in love at 13? Come on now, does she even know what love is? I totally understand the sentiment because that was my initial thought. I can tell you that this young girl's parents shared your sentiment because when the love of her life caught the eye of another little girl in school and broke up with her, they told their heartbroken daughter that she should just get over it, that she wasn't really in love to begin with. They didn't consider what she was going through as true loss and figured she'd be fine. A few days later, that heartbroken tween girl committed suicide.

That can't be right; I hear you thinking. Suicide over such a trivial loss is such a tragedy, and you'd

be correct about that. The problem here, however, is
considering her loss trivial. Yes, for us, that loss *is*
insignificant; we probably can remember the crushes
that we had in middle school, high school and
college and remember how fleeting they all were.
But for her, the loss was devastating. I know this
because I had two acquaintances in college commit
suicide after break-ups. They were picturing life
with their significant other, picturing marriage,
children, and home ownership, and when that
person broke up with them, that life in their mind
ended. They couldn't think past the present without
them.

When we talk about loss, our mind usually goes
to death, divorce, job loss, or house loss. I believe we
all have dealt a lot with death over the last couple of
years and it has been difficult. These are what we
consider devastating losses and they are. It takes
time and emotional effort to recover from any one of
these losses, and trying to comfort someone going
through one or more of these losses is not easy.
Most times, we don't know what to say. Most times,
the person going through the loss knows that there
are no magic words to get them through something,
so being with them through the painful time is
sometimes the only thing we can do. We have to
allow them to grieve in their own way for as long as
it takes. The mistake comes when we think these
life-altering losses are the only losses that deserve
our attention. Even though we didn't feel that the
tween girl's loss was important, it was important
and devastating to her. What we lose is important,

but how we feel about what we have lost is equally important. A loss can be a loved one leaving, but it could be the loss of a position at school. Loss could be losing the ability to walk and realizing a dream will not come true.

As a father, we need to understand that our children may experience losses that we might not consider important. If any of our children consider that loss important, though, we need to help them, giving the loss the weight it deserves. Your child may look back at that moment and realize that the loss they experienced was not all that important in the grand scheme of things, but they'll also remember that you took the time to love on them when they thought it was.

This is what God does; **in Psalms 34:18, it says that "The Lord is nigh unto them that are of a broken heart; and saveth such as be of a contrite spirit." (KJV)** God comforts us regardless of our losses; He wants to help us through our broken-heartedness no matter the reason. As the Great Comforter, He wraps you in His arms and whispers to you that He has you and will not let you go. This is how we need to be to our children. We have to let them know, through word and action, that whatever they lose, we will be there for them, and we will not let them go.

Let's Pray

Lord, I know that everyone in my family may experience loss of one kind or another. I ask you now that you give me the empathy to understand the losses that I don't feel are important, but that are important to my loved ones. Increase my compassion for others and give me the words to say to help them through difficult times. Send the Comforter, the Holy Spirit, down to fill our household and bring us peace that passes all understanding. In Your name we pray, amen.

FAMILY LOSS

We all will mourn due to loss at some point in life. Mourning may be seen in a young child who lost her favorite doll or a senior who lost another old friend. We may mourn because Alzheimer's disease has taken away the mind of our parent or grandparent or because a loved one was separated from us through death. We may mourn because of opportunities we allowed to pass by or because of the time we wasted in our youth that we can never retrieve. We may mourn over situations we messed up ourselves or mourn about the messed-up situation we're in that we had no control over. However you slice it, we all will mourn.

I remember just standing in the shower one day, water running and tears flowing just days after my failed marriage ended in divorce. I had moved to a new place since I lost the home I had once lived in. I lost neighbors with whom I had made friends. I lost finances, furniture and my marital status. I don't know how long I was in the shower; I do remember being pruned as I dried off.

I was in mourning. I was in an emotional place where I didn't want to be and didn't understand. See, I had been sad before, but this was more than a feeling of sadness. This was a place where joy was hidden. This was a place that seemed to have no doors or windows as if no way of escape. I thought it ironic that the word "mourning" shares the same sound and syllables as "morning" when the sun shines through the windows and fresh air fills the skies. But I had no way on my own strength to trade one for the other, to trade mourning for morning.

I prayed as the towel soaked up the water off my skin along with the still streaming tears when I remembered **Matthew 5:4, "Blessed are those who mourn, for they shall be comforted" (KJV)**. I wanted that verse so much, but I didn't believe I had a right to it. After all, I was mourning because of a divorce, not something desperately tragic. No one was severely sick, no one had a tragic accident, no one had died. Matthew 5:4 was not for me, was it?

As I re-read the verse, I realized that there was no stipulation on the word mourn. It did not say, blessed are those who mourn specifically because of illness, or blessed are those that mourn only because of an accident. Matthew 5:4 simply says, "Blessed are those who mourn, for they shall be comforted. It was me who was limiting the power of this verse in my life, not God. I lost something important, and I was mourning. This verse was for me. I was mourning and Jesus said I would be comforted. It didn't matter why I was mourning. Jesus was ready to comfort me.

As I said in the beginning, we will all experience loss. Each loss may be different, and each family member may handle that loss a little differently. The good news is that Jesus is ready to comfort you and your family through whatever loss is encountered. After all, there is no hurt that Jesus does not understand. In times when loss comes, remember Matthew 5:4. Whatever loss your family is experiencing, teach your children to pray, and allow Jesus to move you from mourning to morning in the light of His love.

Let's Pray

Dear Lord, we thank you for staying so close to us when we have lost things we loved. You gave us your word to remind us that you too have shed tears and felt the depth of anguish mourning brings. We thank you that your word promises to comfort our mourning and that one day you will come and take us to heaven where we will never mourn again. In Jesus' name, Amen.

FAMILY PRIDE

As Christians, when we hear the word "pride," most of us will go straight to Proverbs and its many warnings regarding pride, the most famous of which is "pride goeth before a fall." These are very true words and there are many situations where pride can cause problems in a family from a father's perspective.

One main area is how we interact with our children. As a parental figure and the priest of the home, we have a specific position in the family that is vitally important. However, we are still human and are prone to human error. Mistakes can happen and we might find it difficult to not only acknowledge a mistake, but to apologize for it. Our pride fights mightily against us doing this and will push us to come up with every excuse in the book not to apologize, even bringing up totally unrelated issues to put ourselves in the right once again. I can clearly say that this is the enemy talking. Just because we're the head of the household doesn't mean that we do not apologize for mistakes we make. Only a bad leader claims never to be wrong and to never make mistakes; only Christ is perfect. Apologizing, especially to our children, might be a blow to our pride, but there are benefits to doing so. Our sons will learn to be gracious and to acknowledge their mistakes; their future wives will thank you. Our daughters will learn how a good man acts and will avoid possible mates who never say they're sorry.

This also goes for our interactions with our wives. There was one incident where my wife asked me to take something out of the oven. I opened the oven, grabbed the aluminum pan of macaroni and cheese, and attempted to pick it up. However, I misjudged the weight, and I didn't have a good grip on it and I dropped it on the open oven door, causing a cheese explosion. It was clearly my fault; my wife was nowhere near me when it happened. However, my pride caused – forced – me to find some way to blame her for what I did. I blamed her for rushing me to take it out, saying, "If you hadn't been pushing me, this wouldn't have happened!" I still cringe, remembering how wrong I was. My wonderful wife did not argue with me, but we both cleaned up the cheese in silence. When I finally pushed myself to apologize, she revealed how much it hurt when I blamed her. There was a lot of cheese everywhere, but I had done more damage with those words than any of the cheese did. Pride can make you do some seriously hurtful things in a marriage and it must be kept in check.

From what we've covered, it looks like pride is a bad thing, but I want to take a moment to highlight the good aspects of pride. Pride works best when it is placed outside of yourself. Like when we're proud of our kids for doing well on a project, or getting a good grade on a test, or even tackling a task or chore without being asked. These are all pride moments, and we must make sure that they know how proud we are of them. This also extends to our wives. Let her know how proud you are to be her husband; how proud you feel when she does anything from cooking a meal to tackling a task at work to deftly handling her office at church. Our pride in our family is an underrated motivator. It works better than anger and yelling.

Lastly, what we should all have pride in is the Lord. **Jeremiah 9:24 says, "But let him that glorieth glory in this, that he understandeth and knoweth me, that I am the Lord which exercise lovingkindness, judgement, and righteousness, in the earth: for in these things I delight, saith the Lord." (KJV)** We should feel pride in knowing God and that His only begotten Son died for our sins. We should feel proud that we are bought with a price and that the most-high God values us. It is important for us and our families to feel that pride.

That kind of pride should obligate us to do what we can for the Lord.

Pride that separates us, which we use to prop ourselves up, is not useful and can damage our familial relationships. However, the pride that brings us together, that motivates us to do more for each other, our fellow man and our church is the kind of pride we should be practicing. That kind of pride will not go before a fall.

Let's Pray

Dear Father, I ask You to help me to root out self-pride from my life. Help me to recognize when my pride is pushing me to do or say something hurtful or unhelpful… and help me to give all glory to You for any and all of my accomplishments. I thank You now for what I have and what I've been able to achieve. Also, help me to open my mouth to celebrate my family members for their accomplishments, big or small. Thank You, Lord. In Jesus' name, amen.

FAMILY PRIDE

"But he gives more grace. Therefore it says, "God opposes the proud but gives grace to the humble." –James 4:6 (NIV)

I watched a British Comedy show called 'Keeping up Appearances,' about a woman who is willing to run rough-shod over her family to keep up a look of having it all together in front of their neighbors, church members, friends, or anyone whom she deems important. She has hidden behind bushes to avoid people seeing her dressed less than perfect. Her antics to keep up these appearances are quite comical but also very tiring and sad when you see how diminished her family feels by her actions.

Although I was watching the television show, I had to question whether I was the star of my own television show about a woman (me) who was attempting to keep up appearances at the expense of her family in her own sense of pride. Did I turn away my children's friends from visiting because my house wasn't perfectly cleaned? Did I refuse to give someone a meal because I thought my cooking was less than perfect? Did I refuse to attend a social event with my husband because my outfit was less than perfect? Unfortunately, the answer to all these questions was Yes! At that time in my life, there was no way I was going to let myself be seen as less than perfect.

Herein lies the problem; I'm not perfect. I was simply trying to keep up an appearance of what I thought was perfect. But at what cost? My children had to play alone. A friend went hungry. My husband missed a nice time out socially. All because I was too proud to be seen as exactly what I am. Imperfect.

Had I accepted the fact that I am imperfect, my house would have been a home where kids could visit and play. My kitchen would be a place where even the simplest meal would fill a hungry belly. And my husband and I could bond over social events as we meet with old friends and make new ones.

The really sad thing is that my pride put me in opposition to the things I wanted most. Pride placed me spiritually in opposition with God. James 4:6 says, " But he gives more grace. Therefore it says, "God opposes the proud but gives grace to the humble."

I want a home where kids can come and hang out with my kids and play and feel comfortable. I want to serve and help those who need a meal or just help with simple basic necessities. I want to fellowship together, especially alongside my husband who doesn't care if my dress is a little wrinkled. My pride was standing in the way of God using me to share His goodness with others in each of these circumstances. Pride is God's enemy and mine.

Thankfully, this bible verse tells us that God gives grace to the humble. When we humble ourselves and teach our children to do the same, we get the blessings of God's grace. **2 Corinthians 12:9 says, "But he said to me, My grace is sufficient for me and, for my power is made perfect in weakness..." (ESV),** God's grace is able to keep us humble, our humility is able to help us obtain God's grace. Its's a beautiful cycle that keeps on going. I am thankful that God will help us to change our prideful ways if we ask him to. Are you trying to keep up appearances? If so, ask yourself what that is costing you. Then ask God to help you overcome your pride and give you the grace He is longing to give you.

Let's Pray

Dear Jesus, I want to live in the place where your grace surrounds me. Give me a humble heart that connects with your grace. Help me to put pride far away so that I become your close friend and never an enemy.

Help my appearance to look more and more like You. In Jesus' name, Amen.

FAMILY FORGIVENESS

As Christians, our lives should revolve around the word forgiveness. Mainly because it's through Christ's sacrifice on the cross that He forgives us of all our sins and cleanses us from all unrighteousness. The essence of the gospel is that no matter what you have done throughout your life, no matter how horrible or heinous, God will forgive you if only you go and ask Him. The Bible says in Micah that those sins are cast into the depths of the ocean and He remembers them not. That kind of forgiveness is life-changing and can soften the hardest of hearts.

What some of us tend to miss is that we are to extend that same forgiveness to others. **Ephesians 4:32 says, "And be ye kind to another, tenderhearted, forgiving one another, even as God for Christ's sake hath forgiven you." (KJV)** Giving forgiveness is just as much a part of our Christian walk as getting forgiveness, and Christ talks about it as an expectation of our interaction with others. One might think that we need to be reminded to forgive strangers, co-workers, or even fellow church members. However, where a lot of us are having a problem upholding this principle is in dealing with our own family members. Many times, we have an easier time forgiving Sis. Johnson than forgiving Aunt Francine. Over time, this lack of forgiveness becomes grudges and extends for years, sometimes decades.

As the fathers or spiritual leaders of our households, it is our job to set the tone as well as show the example that God needs His children, and our children, to see. They need to see us forgiving someone who wronged us outside of the home, and they also need to see us forgiving family members as well. That might look like forgiving our wives when we feel they have wronged us, and that forgiveness includes forgetting, since we are to be following God's example. Back when I was in school, I remember taking tests in a particular class all through a semester; some of those tests I did well, others, not so much. I remember the pure relief that I would feel when the teacher would announce to the class that she was not going to count all the tests, and when it came to calculating our final grade, she wasn't going to count the lowest one. It wasn't that I didn't take the test; I clearly did, it had been graded and recorded. However, for the purposes of my final grade, it was as if that test never took place.

That's what God does with our sins. It's not that we did not commit those sins; we clearly did. But for the purposes of our salvation, it's as if those sins never happened. This is the same type of forgiveness we need to extend to others, especially our family members. Forgiveness is not keeping quiet about something they did until it will work well in an argument later. Forgiveness is not accepting someone's apology but ripping them apart to others behind their back. Forgiveness is acting as if that wrong never happened.

We need to ensure that our homes are places of forgiveness. We need to forgive our spouses and we need to forgive our children as well. We may indeed need to bring up past wrongs, particularly with children, if we are addressing a pattern of behavior that needs to be stopped. However, we need to ask the Holy Spirit to help us balance those actions with true forgiving and forgetting. If children feel that our forgiveness is authentic, they will be more open about things they are experiencing and things they have done. We also do not want to do the enemy's work; he will seek to keep adults and children depressed, reminding us of the things that we have done and telling us that our Creator and those around us would never forgive us. This is why when the Gospel falls on new ears, it is such a weight being lifted off a new believer's shoulders. It is also a weight being lifted from children who feel they will not be accepted because of what they might have done. Receiving forgiveness translates to giving forgiveness, and children that readily forgive grow up to be adults that readily forgive and do not hold on to grudges within the family. Any glimpse that our children have of God must first appear in our home, and it's our job as priests of that home to ensure that the household environment accurately reflects Him.

Let's Pray

Dear gracious and heavenly Father, first I ask that you forgive me for the wrongs and sins that I have committed. Help me to put away bad thoughts and evil intentions as well as to make a concerted effort to walk uprightly. I thank you for your infinite grace to forgive even me. Lord, help me to extend this same forgiveness to others, especially my family. Help me to truly forgive and forget, allowing my love for them to be seen more clearly. I pray this in Jesus' name, amen.

FAMILY FORGIVENESS

Everything was ready! The room was decorated with Mickey Mouse characters on the wall and a "Welcome Home" banner. The basinet was assembled with a whimsical mobile attached and soft comfy linens draped in it. There was a sturdy changing table filled with diapers, wipes, lotions, and powders. Onesies, tiny t-shirts, bibs, and blankets were neatly folded in the dresser. We anticipated everything we would need for our little one's debut into our world.

I can recall having multiple discussions with my husband about the baby's arrival. We talked about how to handle things when the baby would not sleep at night, what to do, when to do it, who would do it. We discussed what to do if the baby became ill, which illness we would treat with natural remedies and when prescription medications would be best.

We asked and answered every question imaginable; how to keep the baby away from the wood stove, when to take him for his first haircut, who we will trust to babysit, the list went on and on; we were ready. We knew the baby was coming. We knew that there were going to be challenges. We knew it might even be difficult at times. But we were ready to love this baby unconditionally; our game plan was set.

Just as there is an anticipation of joy in a family when a new baby is about to arrive, there is something else that needs to be anticipated. Family members are flawed, and flawed people cause hurt. Family members may hurt you. Hurt within the family must also be anticipated.

Colossians 3:13 says, "13 Make allowance for each other's faults, and forgive anyone who offends you. Remember, the Lord forgave you, so you must forgive others." (NLV)

It is the worst feeling when the ones closest to you hurt you. But God tells us in his word to expect it. He tells us to make an allowance for it, show tolerance, and then forgive it. When we realize that hurt will come, we can make a game plan, a plan to allow God to heal the hurt and bring our hearts to the place where we can forgive. There are some hurts that can be easily forgiven; siblings teasing each other, an unthoughtful word said in haste, even an unkind word said in anger. Other hurts may take more time to forgive; an act of infidelity, a betrayal. Whatever the hurt, forgiveness needs to happen, if not for the one who hurt you, for yourself.

God also reminds us in this text that He has forgiven us for hurting Him. I can't imagine what the size of a heart would be if it had to hold all of the forgiveness that God has given to me, to us! But I can imagine the scene on the cross where Jesus stretched his arms as wide as He could and shed His blood to forgive us of our sins. Christ knew from the foundation of the world that you and I would sin. He made a game plan before He even created man. He made an allowance for the hurt, the sin against Him. He showed tolerance, patience, and mercy. He lovingly forgave us. How I wish I could be more like Jesus and forgive so freely. But through Him, there is victory in the forgiveness arena. There is healing for every hurt.

Christ wants us to be saved. He wants us to return to Heaven one day, where there will be no more hurts. But He also knows that there is no place for unforgiveness in our heavenly home, so he stands waiting for us to turn our hurts over to Him. He wants families to thrive in love and forgiveness.

Have a family discussion about forgiveness. Talk about a game plan when hurt occurs. Ask the question; Is there anyone in the family that needs to forgive today? Pray as a family for the ability to forgive. Be ready to forgive unconditionally. Have your game plan set.

Let's Pray

Dear Jesus, thank you for extending your hands on the cross to forgive us for the sins we committed against you. Even now, your forgiveness towards us has not been exhausted. Just as you forgive us, help us to be ready to forgive others. Lord, you asked us to forgive, help us to do as you ask. In Jesus' name, Amen.

Theme 2 NOTES

THEME 3 – RENOVATION AND EXPANSION

Over time, almost every home will need to be updated in order to continue to fill the needs of those that live there. Sometimes areas might need to be slightly changed, some others might need to be largely expanded. Every family grows, and with that growth, needs and expectations will change. It is best to be prepared for that growth so that provision can be made for it, and each member of the family can expand and thrive. This section of the devotional will walk you through the topics of Family Motivation, Family Gifts and Talents, Family Finances, Family Labor and Family Advancement.

FAMILY MOTIVATION

I've held two types of jobs in my life. The first
type is where I felt like an interchangeable cog in a
vast machine, and nothing I did ultimately mattered.
If I didn't lend my expertise and abilities, someone
else easily could fill my shoes and accomplish the
task without question. However, the second type of
job is where I felt that what I did made a difference.
I contributed to a final product that might still have
come to fruition without my expertise and abilities;
however, it would have been different and it might
have taken a lot longer. I can tell you that getting up
in the morning to go to the first type of job was
difficult. Would it really matter if I wasn't there? It
took considerable effort not to burn yet another
vacation or sick day and pull the covers over my
head. The second type of job was different, though.
I knew what difference I made. I knew that if I

wasn't there, a number of tasks might not get done, and some other tasks would be delayed. I was also blessed enough that my work and expertise were greatly appreciated in a couple of these jobs. Getting out of bed was easier when I had the second type of job. You can say I was motivated to go.

When we talk about motivation, thoughts extend past employment and inevitably land on life itself. It is easy to look at everything that we are called on to do, everything we are supposed to be and become overwhelmed. I've been there; some days, I felt like the best course of action was to pull the covers over my head. Looking back at it, I have to admit to myself that I was experiencing depression. I felt like I wasn't important and I didn't matter; just an insignificant speck on an insignificant planetary speck in a vast universe. What I did didn't matter in the grand scheme of things, and my happiness was not high on anybody's list of priorities.

I have since realized how wrong I was. I also realized that it was the enemy whispering in my ear that whole time. I matter. *We* matter. Particularly in the eyes of the Lord. Not only did God specifically create us, He *planned* us. We are not mistakes or surprises when it comes to God; He meant for us to be here. We also fit specifically into God's plan; He has this grand, intricate plan to save man, to bring happiness to the world…He looked at that plan, saw a role that was needed, and designed us, with our abilities and talents, to fit it. And He knew we would not be perfect; He knew we would screw some stuff up, and He made us anyway.

Our happiness is also a priority to the Lord. **Jeremiah 29:11 says, For I know the plans I have for you," says the Lord. "They are plans for good and not for disaster, to give you a future and a hope." (NLT)** God's plans for us are not only for His benefit, they are for ours. The plan He charts for us takes our happiness into account. He knows what will make us truly happy; He created us after all.

Motivating our children should take a similar path to what God tells us in his word. Our children should be regularly told how special they are, that God created them for a reason, that God has a plan for them that will not only make God happy but will make them happy as well. That nobody else can carry out that plan as well as they can. Through prayer, study and observation, our job should be to realize what path God wants us to take, and them as well.

One of my favorite passages in the Bible is **Isaiah 40:31, "But those who trust in the Lord will find new strength. They will soar high on wings like eagles. They will run and not grow weary. They will walk and not faint." (NLT)** Trust in the Lord to carry you through, to set a course for your life, to plan for your happiness. The strength that you gain from knowing that you are following God's plan for your life will make you feel like you can take on the world. That's more than enough to get you out of bed in the morning.

Let's Pray

Dear heavenly Father, I am so thankful that You didn't just make me, but that You planned me, designed me…You specifically wanted me here. Thank You for knowing beforehand that I would make mistakes, yet making me and loving me anyway. Help me, Lord, to be motivated to be about Your business…excite me, Lord! Help that excitement to be contagious throughout my entire family, and help us all to be motivated to not only go through our day-to-day tasks, but to reach higher and incredible heights with You. In Jesus' name, amen.

FAMILY MOTIVATION

"But they who wait for the LORD shall renew their strength; they shall mount up with wings like eagles; they shall run and not be weary; they shall walk and not faint." –Isaiah 40:31 (ESV)

You guys are crazy! That was what my husband and I heard from family, friends, and sometimes even our own thoughts when we decided to move from New York to Alabama. Alabama was the last place either of us wanted to live (no offense to Alabamians). We felt the Lord was impressing us to move for the sake of our son's education, so we decided to move. To make the situation even crazier, my husband was downsized from his job six months before we were to move.

Our well-meaning family and friends thought we should stop and rethink the move, or maybe just sit still and make sure we were following what the Lord was telling us to do and not what we wanted ourselves. They wanted us to stand still.

But standing still was not what we needed to do at that time. Standing still would have been detrimental during that time. Believe me when I say that hubby and I did not want to move to Alabama at all! We were not financially ready to move. Our home in New York was not ready to sell, my own job was transitioning, and hubby did not have a job at all. Staying put did seem like the logical thing to do under those circumstances.

Isaiah 40:31 says, "They that wait on the Lord, shall renew their strength, they shall mount up on wings as eagles, they shall run and not be weary, they shall walk and not faint."

At first glance, it would seem that our family and friends were right. This verse says to wait on the Lord. Wait, as in stand still and see what the Lord will do. Wait, and see what door the Lord will open. Wait, don't move until the Lord tells you. All of this may be true in most circumstances, but this verse was saying a little something different to us.

Hubby and I had already stood still when we enrolled our youngest son in the only school of our faith even remotely near to us for his primary education. The closest high school of our denomination was a boarding school in Pennsylvania. Once he completed his K-8 education, our options for high school were to send him far away, send him to public school, or home-school him. But there was one more option; we all move near a high school of our faith and take him to school there each day. This last option was the one we believed the Lord was leading us to do. We did not need to stand still and see, we needed to move. When I re-read Isaiah 40:31, the verse says to wait, but waiting does not always mean standing still. This is actually a motivating verse.

When a runner is on the field for a long-distance run, she knows that eventually she will become tired, but she also knows that stopping at the first sign of tired is not the best way to help her win the race. Instead, she keeps running; she keeps moving because she is waiting for something to happen. She is waiting for that burst of adrenaline to kick in and give her that extra energy to help her soar around the track.

For hubby and I, while we waited for the Lord to open doors for the move, hubby patched holes and fixed wires in our house, prepping it for sale. While we waited, I packed clothing and cabinet items. While we waited, we researched the area we planned to move to for fun things to do there. While we waited, we kept on moving until the Lord renewed our strength with His Godly adrenaline and allowed us to soar to Alabama.

Within months of our listening to the Lord's leading and ever so gently pushing back on family voices and opinions, we were living in Alabama. It did not take long before hubby and I were settled in, both working and watching our son thrive in his new high school. It was a perfect fit for us.

Is God telling you and your family to do something, go somewhere, create something? What are you waiting for? A better question is, how are you waiting? Standing still is one way. But allowing Isaiah 40:31 to motivate you into working, doing, serving while you wait on the Lord to help you mount up, soar, run and never get tired, is amazing.

Let's Pray

Our Father, you are the orchestrator of our lives. Help us to know your voice and listen for your cues to move or to stand still. In doing so, you will cause us to soar all the way to heaven with you. In Jesus' name, Amen.

FAMILY GIFTS AND TALENTS

Okay, I'm willing to admit it; I'm envious of my wife. Sherri is an intelligent, funny, and amazing woman, but I'm envious of her awesome singing voice. My wife could stand up in front of the church and belt out a song regardless of accompaniment, and she has been known to bring some members of the congregation to their feet. As for yours truly, my singing voice was never meant to stand out by itself, which is why it is usually tucked into the back of a chorus of voices in a choir if it's heard at all. On more than one occasion, I have longed for that voice that sounds as good as I pretend it sounds when I'm in the shower or in my car by myself.

I doubt I'm alone; nearly everyone I know wishes they were better at something. More often than not, it is the type of talent that gets noticed and receives accolades from everyone. Unfortunately, it is not difficult to make the jump from wishing for better talents to thinking that we don't have gifts or talents at all. Some of us believe we've gotten the short end of the stick when it comes to that department. We look at some of the people around us and say that it would be nice if God blessed us with any talent at all. There are times when such sentiments can lead to depression.

What we need to keep in mind, however, is that God gave *everyone* a gift or talent. **1 Corinthians chapter 12** is all about those gifts and talents and how each one is important, but the verse that needs to be highlighted is **verse 7: "But the manifestation of the Spirit is given to each one for the profit of all." (NKJV)** Every person has been given a measure of the Holy Spirit which is a talent or gift of some sort; no, you're not the one person who got passed over. Sometimes it's just a matter of finding out what that talent is.

As fathers, we will undoubtedly hear from our children that it would be awesome if they could do X, Y or Z. Being that we know that everyone can do something well, or even extremely well, our children will be good at something, or even a bunch of things; and God is so awesome that not only will they be good at that something, they most likely will enjoy doing it too. The hardest part of this is locating this talent. We need to expose our children to a lot of different things and encourage them to try things they may be reluctant to try. They may find they actually have quite a number of talents. No, not every talent will put them up in front of many people getting praise, but that doesn't make the talent less important. God needs behind-the-scenes people as well as up-front people.

This thought was brought home to me one day when our oldest needed help with his accounting homework. He was confused about his assignment and came to me about it. I knew absolutely nothing about accounting at the time, but I told him to give me an hour to digest the chapter he was studying, after which I was able to help him understand what he was struggling with. It didn't really occur to me at the time, but I was using my gift of teaching, which has become more evident over the years. My wife later said she was envious of my ability to do that. Envious of me?! She's the one with the phenomenal singing voice! However, I realized how important each gift is to the people around us, to our church and our world. God gave each one of us a talent or gift for a reason; He needs us to exercise that talent or that gift and put it into use to further His kingdom. If we don't yet know what that talent is, it's time to get into prayer and try things that might be out of our comfort zone. At the end of the day, we might not be doing things for an audience of hundreds, but I love the idea of doing things for God's audience of one.

Let's Pray

Dear Father in heaven, thank You for the gifts and talents that You've given me. Point me in the right direction as I try to help my family and myself realize what talents we might have. Lord, help us to be humble; to always remember, no matter what praise we may receive from the performance of our talents, that ultimately all praise belongs to You. Help us to use them in the way You intended. In Jesus' name, amen.

FAMILY GIFTS AND TALENTS

"1 Then the LORD said to Moses, 2 "See, I have chosen Bezalel son of Uri, the son of Hur, of the tribe of Judah, 3 and I have filled him with the Spirit of God, with wisdom, with understanding, with knowledge and with all kinds of skills. 6 Moreover, I have appointed Oholiab son of Ahisamak, of the tribe of Dan, to help him. Also I have given ability to all the skilled workers to make everything I have commanded you." –Exodus 31:1-3, 6 (NIV)

When God wanted His meeting tent and the ark of the covenant made, He called the experts in to do it. God chose Bezalel and Oholiab as his workmen. God knew they were experts because God himself gave them the expertise. God knew all about the job that He wanted done. He knew what it would take to get the job right. He knew who He had equipped for such a task.

There was an occasion when my husband, Clinton, was asked to give a children's story for a youth rally in Albany, NY. My husband had done many children's stories in church and accepted the invitation without hesitation. There was nothing unusual about my husband giving the story, but I remember feeling an uneasiness about it. There was something out of place about it, and I was not sure why I felt that way. That night I tried not to think about it anymore and went to sleep. I woke up the next morning and chuckled a little about what God had shown me about that feeling. I fully understood why I was apprehensive about the children's story.

What God helped me understand was that even though the rally coordinator asked Clinton, my husband, to give the children's story, God wanted Clinton, my son to give the story. The rally coordinator chose my husband, but God knew all about the job He wanted done. God knew what it would take to get the job done right. God knew who he had equipped for the task.

As I looked at my youngest son, I thought about the work my husband and I had poured into him. Reading the Word with him, praying with him, encouraging him to recite bible memory verses in church, and participating in youth services. I also thought about the things that God had poured into him. His courage, his ability to learn and retain things, his willingness to do things for Jesus. His little 5-year-old body was brimming with gifts and talents.

After some preparation, young Clinton gave the children's story at the youth rally that day in front of a federation of churches. He told the story of Elisha and the she-bears (he tempered the scary parts), and he prayed for all the young children who attended the rally.

God used little Clinton's gifts and talents to expertly spark a new generation of workers in the church. We soon noticed young children giving the children's story at their own churches and adults allowing younger children to serve in more areas in the church. There were 5- and 6-year-olds praying for offering, leading little choirs for special music, and preaching little sermonettes!

God tells us that he equips each of us with gifts and talents. God also has a job for each of us to do. Assess the gifts and talents in the family. Ask God what jobs the family can do. Allow God to choose his experts in the family. Then go do all that He has commanded you as He blesses!

Let's Pray

Dear Jesus, how wonderfully you equip each of us with gifts and talents. You give us expertise to use to better mankind, and to bring glory to your name. Help us to learn to use what you have placed in us to further your kingdom. In Jesus' name, Amen.

FAMILY FINANCES

"Lord, if You give me a million dollars, that would solve all my problems! I'll even tithe 10…no, 15% to the church, so it's a win/win for You and me! If I get that million, I'll be at church bright and early *every* week!" Unfortunately, there's very few Christians who haven't prayed or even thought of some version of this prayer at some point in time. To be honest, I was one of those Christians, actually wondering if I should play the lottery so I can pray about winning. I have since realized that this is a completely wrong approach, and not only because one needs to be really careful when we promise God something in exchange for something else.

I realized that if I'm asking God for money, I'm actually limiting how God can bless me with what I actually want. We usually want the money for something specific. I've found it is better to cut out the middle man of money and pray directly for what I'm looking for. God may gift you with the money you need, or He may gift you with a reduction of the cost of said item so you can afford it with the money you currently have on hand. God may even decide to upgrade what you're looking for because you are actually thinking too small.

Let's be honest; sometimes we ask God for money because we want to buy things that we don't believe God would actually give us. Or at the very least, we think that what we want wouldn't be high on the list of God's priorities. First of all, it's silly to think that God wouldn't be reading your intentions, so praying for money to do things God wouldn't approve of isn't fooling anyone. Also, you'd be surprised what fits into God's list of priorities. You, your family, and your collective happiness will always be important to the Lord. **Matthew 6:33 says, "But seek ye first the kingdom of God, and his righteousness, and all these things will be added onto you." (KJV)** God knows how to bless his children with the things they need and many of the things they want.

Unfortunately, there will be some of us who will not experience the full extent of God's generosity because we do not return a faithful tithe and offering. The bible in Malachi 3:10 is very clear; if we bring our tithe to the storehouse, God is promising to open the windows of heaven and pour us out such a blessing that there will not be room to receive it. We have experienced this first hand; God has put employment opportunities in our laps when we weren't even looking for them, He has pointed my wife to sales that she wasn't expecting, God even extended the life of the items we use so that we didn't need to replace them as quickly. Serving the Lord and giving what He has asked us for will always benefit us more than it benefits Him.

As fathers, we need to make sure our children understand the concept of asking for the items that we need and want instead of asking for a pile of money, and they need to see it in practice. Pray for the items the family needs during family worship; help them to pray for anything they are looking for. When God grants these requests, let's make sure to acknowledge with our children that God has come through and answered their prayers. Then make sure to thank God in prayer with them. Also, make sure they understand the concept of tithing; God gave them the money they have, and He is asking for a portion back. We found it best to tell our children that a tenth of what they earned isn't theirs to begin with; that it belongs to God and they are to give it back to Him when they get the opportunity to do so.

God knows what you need and He knows what you want. Let Him worry about those things; you can pray for what you need or want and then focus on serving Him. You'll be surprised how often He comes through and blesses you.

Let's Pray

Dear heavenly Father, I ask you to change my mindset when it comes to money. Help me to put You first when it comes to our finances, remembering to return a faithful tithe and offering. Help my family and I to be good stewards of the funds that You've allowed us to have, and to always give thanks to You for it. Also, help us not to limit You by asking for money; remind us to ask for the things we need and allow You to bless us any way You want. Thank you, Lord, amen.

FAMILY FINANCES

While strolling through memory lane, I remembered as a little girl asking my father for some money. I held out my hand, expecting a nice round quarter. My dad reached into his pocket and put a shiny round nickel in my palm. I looked at the nickel and then up at my father with as much disappointment as my face could convey. Seeing the disappointment in my little face, my father took back the nickel and put it in his pocket. I waited for his hand to emerge out of his pocket again with a quarter. Instead, my father just walked away. He left me standing there with no quarter and no nickel.

That was a pretty hard lesson for a 5-year-old, but it remains with me even to this day. My father was teaching me to be content with what I am given. I was not entitled to a quarter or even a nickel and should have been thankful for what I received. My father wanted me to learn to be grateful. That's what our Father in Heaven wants us to learn as well.

Most often, when talking about finances, we hear about saving money, the ills gambling and pyramid schemes, and the duty of returning a faithful tithe, all of which is important. But two things are also important concerning finances.

First of which is being grateful for what you are given. Being content with the things that God has blessed you with.

¹⁹ Also, every man to whom God has given riches and possessions, He has also given the power *and* ability to enjoy them and to receive [this as] his [allotted] portion and to rejoice in his labor—this is the gift of God [to him]. Ecclesiastes 5:19 (AMP)

God is amazing every time he blesses us and then gives us the ability to enjoy his blessings. In other words, being content with God's blessings is a choice that He gives us the power to make. When a financial blessing is bestowed on us, the size of that blessing does not determine our contentment; we do. God's gift is not just the blessings but also the ability to enjoy the blessing!

Unfortunately, we see people who have large financial accounts, some too large to spend in a lifetime, but are unhappy, discontent, and miserable. This is not what God wants for his children. This is not what God wants for your family. God wants your family to receive and enjoy all that you are given.

Secondly, we are to be a blessing to others through our finances. Just as our God is a giver, God wants us to be givers too. When Covid-19 first hit and the country was going on lockdown, I was listening to a news report about people losing their jobs and having a difficult time paying for their prescription medications. My husband and I decided to use some of our little savings to help out. We took what we could afford to a pharmacy and requested to pay for as many prescriptions as possible with what we gave. We don't know for whom or how many prescriptions were paid, but we knew that God wanted us to give generously. We were happy to give and we know that we have been blessed because of it.

2 Corinthians 9:6-8 (NLT) says, [6] Remember this—a farmer who plants only a few seeds will get a small crop. But the one who plants generously will get a generous crop. [7] You must each decide in your heart how much to give. And don't give reluctantly or in response to pressure. "For God loves a person who gives cheerfully."[a] [8] And God will generously provide all you need. Then you will always have everything you need and plenty left over to share with others.

Financially saving, staying away from gambling and get rich quick schemes is smart; returning a faithful tithe is commanded, but having a family that is thankful for what God gives them financially and willing to give to others cheerfully is ripe for God's blessings.

Let's Pray

Dear Jesus, you have blessed us beyond what we deserve, and we thank you. You are pleased when we are grateful for the blessings we receive so help us to receive each blessings with thanksgiving. We ask Lord, that you help us to be a blessing to others as well, giving cheerfully as a reflection of your love. In Jesus' name, Amen.

FAMILY LABOR

There is a saying that my father has said multiple times throughout my life; I can almost call it his motto or a principle he lived by. He would say, "Whatever you do, do it to the best of your ability." He drummed this into me repeatedly, and now I find that I have been saying it to my own sons. I was pretty young when I began hearing this, so it wasn't until I was older and had done a fair bit of bible study that I realized he was paraphrasing **Ecclesiastes 9:10a: "Whatever your hand finds to do, do it with your might." (NKJV)** This meant that no matter how small or meaningless you believe the task to be, you still make an effort to ensure it's done right and done well. This established my work ethic very early in life and defined my approach to labor.

The word "labor" is not usually attached to happy thoughts. Biblically, we might think of Jacob laboring 7 hard years for who he thought was Rachel, getting Leah instead and then laboring another 7 years for Rachel. We might think of hours of yardwork under a hot sun. We might even think of the process of bringing a child into the world, a pain I won't even begin to say that I understand. Whatever thought goes through our minds when we think of labor, it's not something we'd usually choose if given the option.

However, we need to alter our thinking when it comes to labor. In the case of Jacob, the bible says that those 7 years felt like only a few days because of his love for Rachel. When we think about those hours of yardwork, we look forward to a point in the near future when the lawn looks great. Even when we talk about childbirth, Christ actually says in John 21 that after a baby is born, the mother forgets about the pain because of the joy of the child she now has. The feelings surrounding labor change when we shift our focus away from the work itself and to what the end result will be when that work is concluded.

Even when we're talking about work that doesn't directly benefit us, we can get joy from how we make others feel. I do a fair amount of housework, not because I find it extremely enjoyable, but because I love how it makes my wife feel when she sees it and knows she doesn't have to do it herself. This labor falls into the category of service, which is something that Christ wants us to do for our fellow man, even someone we might not know. This is the labor that represents Christ's hands and feet; we are doing His work when we are in service to others, which is an incentive to do the absolute best we can since we're representing Him.

The joy of service needs to be awakened in all of us, and it's never too early to start to orient our children's thoughts in that direction. First, help them take the focus off the work itself and shift it to the end result. It helps to rave over a finished task, saying how wonderful the finished product is and how proud you are of them because they completed it. They won't only have the finished product that they can look forward to; it will also be the happiness of their parents they'll enjoy. When we transition to service, we can tell them that not only are we proud of them when they do something for others but that Jesus is even happier than we are. We would tell our children that Jesus is up in heaven, bragging about them to the angels: "That's my child that just did that!"

Lastly, one thing to consider about labor and service is that we might not get a parade in our honor, get mentioned in someone's remarks, or even hear a thank you. However, our Father in heaven sees what we do in private and Jesus says in **Matthew 6:4, "That thine alms may be in secret: and thy Father which seeth in secret himself shall reward thee openly." (KJV)** Believe me, I think we can all agree that getting a thank you from Jesus

Himself when we see him face to face will be better than absolutely anything we get down here.

Let's Pray

Dear Jesus, give me the desire to do service for others, for the people that You love and point me toward. Help me to not seek out praise for the things I do, but to seek to make You happy with my service. Help me to instill the need for service in my family, and help us to be Your hands and feet as we serve others. And help us to curb complaining and focus on the end result. Amen.

FAMILY LABOR

"There is nothing better for a man, than that he should eat and drink, and that he should make his soul enjoy good in his labour. This also I saw, that it was from the hand of God." –Ecclesiastes 2:24 (KJV)

Employment, work, job, grind, duty, chores, hustle all fall under the category of labor. Through labor we produce a paycheck, food from a garden, a clean house, a groomed yard, a written book, a recorded song: production is the result of labor. The concept of labor comes from the foundation of the world. God gave man labor. In Adam's case, he had the job of maintaining the Garden of Eden. **Genesis 2:15 (KJV), "And the Lord God took the man, and put him into the garden of Eden to dress it and to keep it."**

Before sin, Adam's garden-work was pleasant and easy to do. After sin, things got a little labor-intensive. **Genesis 3:17b-19a (NIV), "Cursed is the ground because of you; through painful toil you will eat food from it all the days of your life. [18] It will produce thorns and thistles for you, and you will eat the plants of the field. [19] By the sweat of your brow you will eat your food..."**

It's the "by the sweat of your brow" thing that I think people focus on the most. Yes, sin causes labor to be laborious but that should not be our focus. God tells us in Ecclesiastes that we are most happy when we are able to sustain ourselves through the labor that God gives us.

When my middle son was about 13 years old, he wanted a new pair of sneakers since his old ones were scuffed up and dirty. He saw a particular pair he liked in a local sporting goods store but he didn't have the money for them. I could have easily purchased the sneakers for him, but I had just purchased his old sneakers only a few months ago. He didn't take care of them. So, I decided that if he wanted a new pair, he would have to pay for them himself.

With the understanding that mom and dad were not buying the sneakers, my son went to work. He asked to do extra chores for money. He asked relatives for odd jobs, specifically his grandma, since she pays the best wages. He earned most of the money for the sneakers fairly quickly, but he was still about $10.00 short, even with the sneakers now on clearance. Albeit cash short, I took him to the sporting goods store and talked to him about the power of bargaining. I told him it was a long shot but encouraged him to bargain for the sneakers.

Once in the store, he wasted no time. He walked straight to the shoe department and asked a salesperson to see the department manager. When the manager came out, he looked at me. I pointed to my son and told the manager that he was the customer who asked to speak with him. The manager was quite accommodating and intently listened to what the young patron had to say. My son explained how he worked to save money for a particular pair of sneakers, but he was just a little short. He explained that he was concerned that since the shoes were now on clearance, they would be gone before he could earn enough money to buy them. He asked the manager if he would be willing to discount the sneakers a little more. The manager asked my son to wait while he went into his office. A few minutes passed; the manager came back out and made the deal. My son was able to buy the sneakers with the money he earned.

He wore those sneakers with pride. I watched as he would carefully wipe off his new sneakers and place them back in the box to keep them safe after each wear. This is the "soul enjoying good" that Ecclesiastes is referring to. I reminded my son to thank all of the people that gave him work and to thank God for the strength to work, and for the blessing of the bargain price.

Even though we may not want to labor, God knew that labor is good for us, both young and old. Not just good, but soul enjoying good. From individual jobs to family household chores, we are to be thankful for the labor that God gives us. Then we are to enjoy to the fullest what that labor has produced.

Let's Pray

Our Father in Heaven, you know exactly what makes us happy. You knew before you created us that we would need labor, something productive to do. So we thank you for our labor that brings about production. For in the production, we find enjoyment and satisfaction. In Jesus' name, Amen.

FAMILY ADVANCEMENT

"If you're not moving forward, you're standing still…and if you're standing still, you're falling behind." I have no idea which person or persons to attribute that quote to, but it's a sentiment that has quietly resided in the back of my mind for most of my life. This quote is saying that I need to be working toward or trying to accomplish something at all times and if I'm not, I'm wasting time. Sometimes, I feel uncomfortable relaxing if I haven't done something that I know I should have done. I don't believe I'm alone in how I feel.

I believe this internal desire for advancement or moving toward a goal is God-created. **Proverbs 9:9 says, "Instruct the wise, and they will be even wiser. Teach the righteous, and they will learn even more." (NLT)** God is saying here that even those who count themselves among the wisest or smartest among us should still be striving to learn and accomplish more; you will always have the capacity to continue learning. It might not have to be formal education, it could be learning more about important subjects, but it's good to keep our brains active and not standing idle.

As husbands and fathers, the goals we focus on very well may be our wife's or our children's goals. That was me for many years as I focused my efforts on getting our sons educated and them becoming self-sufficient. I even focused on helping my wife when she decided she wanted to go back to school. However, even though it is noble and needed to make sure your family has goals to reach and to put in effort to assist them in obtaining those goals, do not neglect yourself. For me, my wife finally convinced me (after a good long time) to return to school to get my Masters and I am so glad she did. Sometimes the argument against setting a lofty goal is how long it will take to do it or what age we'll be before we finish; this was my argument. Her counter to that was that I'm going to get to that age anyway; why not get to that age with a Masters? I was worried when I started a graduate program, but I didn't realize how much I missed learning in a classroom setting and enjoying a sense of accomplishment.

We need to instill in our children the importance of setting goals for themselves and that they should be striving for goals in their lives. The flip side of reaching an age and achieving something is finding yourself much older and either not having much to show for it or recognizing that you never attempted to achieve that dream you've had for years. It's a regretful feeling to realize that the time you wasted, you can't get back. We can also show them that it helps them make decisions; if a specific choice does not help or actually lowers their chances of reaching their goal, it should be easy to decide against it. This is the time to make procrastination an enemy; your children will learn from your actions as well as your words, so you need to keep your actions and words in harmony with each other.

The best thing we should teach our children to do is to pray about their goals and pray for those goals to align with what God wants for their lives. He has a plan for every one of us; it's great when our goals and His goals for us are the same. A request for His help in reaching your goals will not fall on deaf ears. God delights in helping us advance and grow in Him at the same time. The great thing about what God wants for us is that whatever skill it requires, He's already put in us.

God is looking for His people to constantly learn, achieve, and advance; as priests of the home, we should want the same for our families. Knowing that you have made steps toward your goal will make whatever rest and relaxation you enjoy that much sweeter.

Let's Pray

Dear heavenly Father, help me to set goals for myself that are in harmony with Your plans for my life. Keep me away from distractions and procrastination, and help me to set a good example for my family. Give me insight and understanding to assist my family in setting their goals, and give me the strength and focus needed to help them reach them. Thank you in advance for being beside us as we strive to reach our goals and to also get to the kingdom. In Jesus' name, amen.

FAMILY ADVANCEMENT

"But I will establish my covenant with you, and you shall come into the ark, you, your sons, your wife, and your sons' wives with you." –Genesis 6:18 ESV

Then the Lord said to Noah, "Go into the ark, you and all your household, for I have seen that you are righteous before me in this generation. –Genesis 7:1 ESV

George W. Bush coined the phrase "No Child Left Behind" when introducing his education policy. I have usurped this phrase and pray each day that No Family is Left Behind when Jesus comes.

My prayer is that as God grows me, my husband, and my children, we will be able to fulfil our purpose in Christ and advance Christ's cause. The advancement of the family, the whole family, is like a musical movement. There is an underlying current of music with different melodic tones running through to create a sound that calls attention to and for Jesus Christ.

Some of the melodic tones are made through educational gains such as a child graduating from kindergarten or college, or financial gains such as a mom or dad getting a promotion at work. There are other advancements that produce high and low tones, like a daughter sewing her first skirt or a son earning money from his first lawn cutting job. Family advancement is about the movement of the family so that no one becomes stagnant or complacent.

God developed our minds to create and produce just as He is the Creator and Producer. It is important for the family to set goals, plans, encourage hobbies, and cultivate talents for all its members. The family will also recognize ways to serve God and each other in doing so.

When my children were young, I was convinced that I had the noisiest home on the block. My eldest son sang all the time; in the house, in the car, at the table, in the shower, and on the toilet. My middle son would bang on everything that could be banged on; tables, pots, countertops, and my thigh if I sat too close to him. My youngest was a talker, I mean every waking moment talker, who also tried to do everything his older brothers did.

My husband and I decided that cultivating these behaviors would work much better than wearing earplugs all day. So, we bought performance tracks for our eldest to sing to. We gave our middle son drum lessons. And we taught our youngest to memorize and repeat scriptures (purposed-talking). As a result, advancement occurred. Our local church gained a singer, a drummer, and a 7-year-old speaker for youth services. My boys gained a creative outlet, confidence, and a sense of accomplishment in Christ. All music to my ears!

I like what God told Noah in the book of Genesis. God was having a conversation with Noah and said, "But I will establish my covenant with you, and you shall come into the ark, you, your sons, your wife, and your sons' wives with you."

God is telling Noah that He is moving him. During the time of Noah, the world was wicked and about to be destroyed. God told Noah it was time to move.

In Genesis 7:1, God continues the conversation, "Then the Lord said to Noah, "Go into the ark, you and all your household, for I have seen that you are righteous before me in this generation."

It is important for the family to make advancements, whether they be educational, through employment or fulfilling hobbies. The family should never stay stagnant or complacent. This also means advancing spiritually and always moving toward Christ who is the undercurrent of the family music. Just as in Noah's time, God is having a conversation with you through His Word. God is telling you and your family to move, to advance toward him. How is your family advancing?

Let's Pray

Dear Lord, you never intend for us to be stagnant, complacent, or unmoving. Help us to use the gifts and talents you have blessed us with to move closer to you, individually and as a family. Thank you for moving us to you. In Jesus' name, Amen.

Theme 3 NOTES

Theme 4 – Finishing Touches

For every house constructed, there are small things that make that house feel like a home. Family pictures, specific furnishings, items that have sentimental value; these are items that make a home feel warmer and lived-in. Even though some might not consider these small items requirements, a family can function with more joy and purpose if attention is paid to these small details. In this final section, the devotional will guide you through the topics of Family Bonding, Family Destination, and Family Worship.

FAMILY BONDING

As technology and services continue to evolve and improve, no one can deny that we are experiencing convenience on levels that we did not anticipate. We can order pizza with a text message, get our groceries delivered to our front door, even purchase a car, used or new, through a website. There are many people that enjoy these services, and there's nothing wrong with that; however, there is something that is increasingly missing as more and more companies go this route: human interaction. It used to be that you had to at least speak to someone on the phone, and now even that is starting to become obsolete. The pandemic has exacerbated this issue, now with "no-contact deliveries" and with many companies opting to let their employees work from home offices.

It is way too easy to allow this condition to permeate our homes. Each family member may be in different rooms, doing their own thing, content to send text messages to each other when interaction is required. This is definitely the case once our children get into their teenage years and one can go hours with never seeing them. Actual in-person interaction becomes difficult and strained, and one might think it easier to not bother. However, family bonding is vital to our children's development.

First of all, God made us social creatures. God could have created Adam and Eve together, but by creating Adam first and allowing him to see how the animal couples paired up and interacted, God instilled in Adam the importance of having a partner, another person to go on life's journey with. Studies have shown that babies that do not get human touch and interaction fail to grow at the same pace as other children and may even end up with physical ailments.

Also, the more we interact with our children, the more comfortable they'll feel talking with us, especially when considering more serious issues. And the more we talk with them, the quicker we will see when something is off about them, prompting us to ask if anything is wrong.

It is very easy for us fathers to be more distant when it comes to our children, especially when they get older. Mothers, in many cases, tend to be the more nurturing of the parents, and many fathers are content to allow their wives to fill that need. It might be uncomfortable for some of us, but it is something we need to push through. Throw your arms around your teenager and hug them for no reason, son or daughter. Take some time and watch some shows and movies they like along with them. Talk with them, laugh with them, bond with them.

Plan time for the family to do things together. For example, my family reclaims Halloween as Family Night, where we do crafts together. We also have a bookshelf filled with board games where we challenge each other to see who will be the winner. Almost always, time gets away from us when we do things together and have fun like this. You may even get children who look forward to game night or family night and want to do it more often.

Romans 12:10 says, "Love each other with genuine affection, and take delight in honoring each other." (NLT) Family bonding should be a joyful experience that children don't grow out of once we can no longer throw them in the air without injuring ourselves. We need to show affection to our wives and our children so they can tangibly feel our love for them. The children from such a household are more grounded, happier and know where to go when they have a problem. God showers us with love and affection; we need to pass some of that on to our families. The home will be brighter for it.

Let's Pray

Dear Father in heaven, I ask You to help our home to be filled with positive interactions between family members. Help us not to drift apart in the same house, but to enjoy spending time in each other's company. For my part, help me to be more affectionate, more personable with my family…and help my actions to encourage other family members to do the same. Thank You in advance, Lord, amen!

FAMILY BONDING

"How good and pleasant it is when God's people live together in unity!" –Psalm 133:1 (NIV)

An iconic moment from the movie Wizard of Oz is when Dorothy clicked the heels of her ruby red shoes together and repeated, "There's no place like home." In truth, there really should be no place like home. Home is more than just where you eat meals, see familiar people, and lay your head at night. Home is where the family is rejuvenated, recharged, relaxed, and refreshed. At least, that's what the goal of the home should be.

Honestly, I remember when my children were young, my home was chaotic, disarrayed, and hectic, far from the relaxed and refreshed model. The kids argued, I yelled, my husband would either referee or retreat from it all. There really was no place like home, but not in a good way.

I found myself taking a step back and reviewing my home in my mind. Remembering what the faces of each family member looked like and the frustration on everyone's brow. I remember praying and asking God to help make my home more peaceful.

Psalm 133:1 says, "How good and pleasant it is when God's people live together in unity!"

Unity was just what my family needed. Sure, we lived together, but we needed to come together in unity. We needed to bond. I turned to the dictionary to get a clear understanding of bonding: the formation of a close relationship, especially through frequent or constant association. Well, we all lived together, so we had frequent and constant association, right? The answer was no. My husband commuted a long way to work and back, so oftentimes when he came home, the kids were already in bed. Not much association there. Our children are spaced far apart in age. We had an older teen, a tween, and a toddler at one time. They all had different interests and different friends. Not much association there. And I spent most of my time with the toddler who needed the most attention. Associations nixed again.

One day I ran across a pretty plaque that read, "Family: like branches on a tree, we all grow in different directions, yet our roots remain as one" (author unknown). I thought about things we all like to do and began implementing family time around them. Movie nights, water wars, and scavenger hunts all worked well. One of the boys' favorites was turning the kitchen into a diner with me pretending to be the owner/waitress. I served homemade "Big Momma Burgers" and the boys would bond over the meal. As I watched them eat in our pretend diner, I could sit back and agree, "How good and pleasant it is when God's people live together in unity!

How your family bonds is as creative as you want it to be. But they need to bond, to serve, play, learn, and worship together. Family bonding is purposeful, not left to chance or simply to the fact that we live in the same vicinity. Jesus was purposeful in connecting with people as He walked and talked and lived with man while on earth. God created us to be social, able to interact with others in a meaningful way. A way that rejuvenates and refreshes so that all the family members will gladly say, "There's no place like home."

Let's Pray

Our Father in Heaven, I want my family to live together in unity. Please make my home a place where my family is revived after dealing with day-to-day life. Help my home reflect your home in heaven until the day when we are able to live with you. In Jesus' name, Amen.

FAMILY DESTINATION

Coming of age in a time before readily-available GPS devices, I prided myself on the ability to read a road map. Even before I got my license, I would pore over maps, working out how to get from point A to point B in what I believed was the shortest amount of time and the least amount of road. When my family would go on cross-country trips, I would sit down with my father and ask him which route we were taking. I would look for opportunities to show my dad a faster way or a shortcut that I had worked out. He began to trust my directions and where I was leading, and during one particular trip, when I suggested an exit that would take 20 minutes off of our time, he went with my suggestion. However, what I didn't know was that, after a windy and lonely road, we would be faced with a closed road with no way to go around. Instead of saving us 20 minutes on the trip, it cost us 30 minutes. My dad reassured me that it was a well-intentioned attempt, but I felt bad nonetheless.

With GPS devices, moments like this are much rarer. Paper maps might be years old, but GPS maps are updated much more often and therefore are a lot more accurate. GPS devices have a much more accurate view of what the roads and the landscape look like, some of them even take traffic patterns into account, and therefore can do a better job of directing us to our destination. This is what I think of when I look at our destinations regarding what the Lord wants from each of us. There are destinations that He wants each of us to reach, and He will always have the best path to get there.

Just like when I had no idea that I was directing my family to a closed road, we would not be able to choose the best path for ourselves or our children without God's help because we have no view of the future. God can see all the pitfalls, detours, closed roads and bottlenecks that will delay or even halt our journeys long before we would have any idea about them. Knowing this, we need to talk to our Creator regularly, asking Him what direction we should be going and what we should be doing. **Proverbs 16:9 says, "A man's heart plans his way, but the Lord directs his steps." (NKJV)** We need to be open to the Lord's leading and learn to determine where He's directing us.

When we speak to our families, particularly to our children, we need to make sure they know that

God does care about our destinations and the paths we take to get there. We also need to keep in mind that the journey might include some pitfalls and setbacks; not every path is perfect and without any problems. Sometimes the evils of this world can impact our journey; sometimes, it's our own stubbornness. However, just like a GPS, our loving Savior will reroute us so we can be on our path once again. Encourage your children to reach out to the Lord regarding their journeys and destinations, and we should too so we can help point them in the right direction.

Ultimately, our journeys need to take us to golden streets and the tree of life. That's where God wants us all to be and He'll be continually rerouting and directing each one of us to make it into the kingdom. Even when we face hardship, wrong turns, and sorrow and loss, we need to commit to following God's path. The destination is more than worth it.

Let's Pray

Dear heavenly Father, please help us, our entire family, to stay on the path that You have laid out for us. Help us not to be discouraged by what the world throws at us, but help us to regularly pray and reach out to You to know which direction to go. Give me insight to the path that You want our children to follow and give me the strength and ability to help them to stay on it. And please, Lord, save us all in your kingdom. I pray in Jesus' name, amen.

FAMILY DESTINATION

"For here we have no lasting city, but we seek the city that is to come." –Hebrews 13:14 (ESV)

"I don't want to clean my room! I'm tired of this place! I'm leaving here!" These were the words from my six-year-old middle son as he packed a little bag to leave our home and live life by his own rules, on his own terms. He had a frustrating day with his big brother being too self-absorbed to pay any attention to him, and now his mom was telling him to do the very thing that takes away all the joy from a boy's day; chores. His little self simply had enough. He was looking to go to a better place where there was no frustration, no troubles, and no chores.

Determined to leave for greener pastures, he said his goodbye with furled eyebrows and walked out the door without even so much as a glance back at me. I could hardly contain myself from laughing, but I knew I had to keep it together for the sake of his dramatic moment. I carefully watched as he stepped off the porch and onto the walkway of our home. After a brief pause, he turned and sat down on one of the front porch steps. I wish I knew what was going through his little mind as he sat there contemplating his new freedom and responsibility.

He returned to the front door and knocked. As I opened the door, he gave me a big hug and said he didn't want to run away. He then carefully articulated his circumstances in the outside world alone. He cried that he was cold and hungry and wanted to be home. He had only been outside five minutes! I gave him the biggest "I love you smile" that I could muster, and all was well again. I handed him a small treat as he happily scooted off to his room to start cleaning, the same chore he previously protested.

I remember feeling just like my little boy; days that were so frustrating I wanted to scream. So many things to do in the day I want to cry. So many awful things happening in the world I felt helpless. I just wanted to pack a bag and run away to a better place.

I'm sure there are times when everyone feels like this. God in his gracious mercy already knew we would have these feelings and He gave us encouragement in Hebrews 13:14, "For we have no lasting city, but we seek the city that is to come."

This earthly home filled with frustrating days is temporary. Sad tears are temporary. The awful things of this world are temporary. There is a better place, a city that is to come. Jesus has prepared a place for me and my loved ones. We often talk as a family about our heavenly home, our forever destination. We talk about what it will be like living on the earth made new, playing with animals that are too fierce here but calm and gentle there. We talk about the Heavenly City, where we will worship God and hear the angels sing. We talk about long hugs with Jesus. As we talk about our destination home, Heaven, I can see the relaxed look on my children's faces. The conversation brings a sense of relief, with not one furled eyebrow in the bunch.

There is something special in knowing that as a family, the desire is that we all wind up together forever. Life will take families to and through many places, some easy and some very hard. How wonderful it is for my family, for your family to seek the city that is to come, the final joyous place; Destination-Heaven!

Let's Pray

Dear Jesus, I thank you for being with me as I go through each day. Sometimes days seems strained and difficult and I want to give up. Thank you for your promise of a better city, a forever-home, a place you lovingly prepared for me and my family, to remind me that my earthly home and its problems are temporary.

*Soon you will come and take us to our promised home-
Heaven. In Jesus' name, Amen.*

FAMILY WORSHIP

A Message to You

From Him: There's been moments where I have found myself awake in bed, unable to sleep and staring at the ceiling or staring into the darkness, depending on how much light was in the room. Many of those times I've found myself reflecting over my past; things I got right, things that I got wrong. What I inevitably find my mind floating toward is what God has done for me, for my family…how He got everything right. Times where He came when I called; times where He acted before I even knew to call for help. I'm amazed that He still deals with me, still uses me, despite my falling short of his ideals. It's those moments I'm reminded of Joshua. Joshua had seen amazing things, had seen God move and even answer prayers that seemed impossible. When he was done and was ready to pass the reigns onto someone else, he gathered the children of Israel, recounted God's amazing works to them and then said in **Joshua 24:15: "Choose you this day whom ye will serve…but as for me and my house, we will serve the Lord." (KJV)** He was convicted; no matter what happened from that point on, he…and his family…was going to serve the Lord. That's what I try to impart to my family…just how great the Lord is and how He is deserving of all of our praise. When we get together, I ask them what they are thankful for…and no matter how small it is, we thank God for it. This is what worship looks like; just praising and praying to Him and recounting how amazing He is. I encourage you and your family to do the same…and not to stop until we can hold His pierced hands and tell him thank you face-to-face.

From Her: **"And the LORD shall make thee the head, and not the tail; and thou shalt be above only, and thou shalt not be beneath, if thou hearken unto the commandments of the LORD thy God which I command thee this day, to observe and to do them." Deuteronomy 28:13 (KJV)** Family worship is where leaders are made. It's the time and space where my husband is the fiercest protector by placing his family at the foot of the One who is all-conquering and all-powerful. Worship is where I am the best nurturer with my children, by cradling them in the arms of the Lord, where they will grow in grace and intelligence. Family worship is where my children learned to become leaders, speaking in the presence of not just a king but The King, learning to articulate their hearts and feelings, and participating in something greater than themselves. Family worship celebrates God, strengthens our commitment to His Word and releases God's promise, "And the Lord shall make thee the head, and not the tail; and thou shalt be above only, and thou shalt not be beneath." What a glorious picture we live out during family worship, as heirs of our Lord and Savior, Jesus Christ.

A PERSONAL PRAYER

Dear Heavenly Father:

Thank you, Lord, for being an amazing God…you hung the sun, moon and stars in the sky…you created all that we see…yet, you take the time to listen to us when we call. Thank you for loving us, and wanting so much to spend eternity with us, that you died on the cross to take away our sins.

Lord, we know that we haven't always been the best examples of your children. Sometimes we don't make time for you. Lord, we repent for the times we have fallen short and ask for your forgiveness. Work on us; help us to be better and more like you.

The ___________________ family thanks you so
(Your family name)
much for all of the things you have done for us.

Thank you for _________________________. Also,
(A blessing God has given you)

thank you for _________________________.
(Another blessing God has given you)

And we can never forget when you

_________________________. You are so
(Something amazing God has done for you)

good to us and we are so thankful for what you've

done and for loving us.

I put the _________________ family, before you
(Your family name)

today. I ask that you would continue to bless

us…and help us to always have love for one another,

as well as love for you. I ask that you would bless

each one of our children, _________________________;
(Your children's name(s))

grow and develop them into the successes that you

have planned for them. Put hedges of protection

around each one of them and keep them from all

harm and all danger.

I also ask that you would strengthen the love

between me and _________________; help us to always
(Your spouse's name)

hold on to each other, even while we hold on to your

unchanging hand. Help us to withstand any and

every attack from the enemy aimed at our marriage

or our family.

Help us, O Lord, to put you first in our endeavors and our decisions…and to be heavenly-minded while outwardly showing your love to others. Help us to be convicted and stay connected to you until you break through the clouds of glory and take us home.

Thank you for your love, your grace and your mercy. Amen.

You are
Cordially Invited

AN INVITATION

We pray that this devotional book has been a blessing to you and your family, and as you've read, maybe you've felt a tugging at your heart. Maybe you haven't given your heart to the Lord… Maybe you've felt that God wouldn't want you anymore because of the things you've done and that your time has passed. We can tell you that nothing is further from the truth. Even if, all this time, you've run away from the Lord, we can tell you that if you stop running and turn around, He is right there. Not right there with a punishment, not right there to chastise you, but right there with His arms held wide, telling you that He never stopped loving you, never stopped pursuing you, never stopped wanting to spend eternity with you. He just wants you to surrender.

Or maybe you did give your heart to the Lord, but that was way back in the past, and since then, you've strayed away and done your own thing. You might have doubted His power or even His existence because of some of the things that you've experienced. It doesn't matter; He still is ready to accept you, wanting an opportunity to show you that He still and will always love you. He wants you to surrender too.

Don't wait until you're cleaned up. Nobody waits to be well before going to the hospital. He'll do all the cleaning that you need if you allow Him in. Let Him do what He wants to do. He wants to save you. Confess your sins to Him…don't worry; He already knows about everything you've done and wants to be with you anyway. Surrender your heart to Him in prayer right now. You know that in this sinful world, tomorrow is not promised. Take the opportunity to do it today. If you need to get baptized, find a bible-believing church and take the plunge. If you are already baptized, find your way back to the pews. In either case, allow Jesus to direct your paths…we promise that you will never, ever regret it.